# Becoming
# Better
# Leaders

To our colleagues in the Maine Network of School Leaders who continue to pioneer their own leadership development. Your experiences, through this book, will inform and inspire others to measure their own leadership effectiveness by their influence on the learning of students in their schools.

# Becoming Better Leaders

## The Challenge of Improving Student Learning

**Gordon A. Donaldson Jr.**
**George F. Marnik**

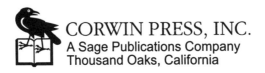

CORWIN PRESS, INC.
A Sage Publications Company
Thousand Oaks, California

*For information address*:

Corwin Press, Inc.
2455 Teller Road
Thousand Oaks, California 91320

SAGE Publications Ltd.
6 Bonhill Street
London EC2A 4PU
United Kingdom

SAGE Publications India Pvt. Ltd.
M-32 Market
Greater Kailash I
New Delhi 110 048 India

Printed in the United States of America

**Library of Congress Cataloging-in-Publication Data**

Donaldson, Gordon, A., Jr.
  Becoming better leaders: the challenge of improving student learning/Gordon A. Donaldson, Jr., George F. Marnik.
    p. cm.
  Includes bibliographical references and index.
  ISBN 0-8039-6181-2 (acid-free paper).—ISBN 0-8039-6182-0 (pbk.: acid-free paper)
    1. Educational leadership—Maine.  I. Marnik, George F.
  II. Title.
  LB2805.D654  1995                                              95-3734
  371.2'009741—dc20

This book is printed on acid-free paper.

95 96 97 98 99 10 9 8 7 6 5 4 3 2 1

Corwin Press Production Editor: Diane S. Foster

# CONTENTS

# PREFACE

**F**ew question the need for better school leadership. Indeed, better schools seem to require better leaders: Improve the leaders and they will lead their schools to better performance. Despite the clarity of this logic, our journeys down this road have so far proven neither straight nor so logically sound. Making better leaders is a complex and little understood process. Moreover, the ways better leaders help create better schools remain mysterious.

Our book depicts the experiences of school leaders as they explored the road to improvement, both for themselves as leaders and simultaneously for their schools' effectiveness with children. They were an unusual caravan, made up of equal numbers of teacher leaders and principals, who melded their own professional growth with specific change initiatives in their schools. Their progress was through learning-in-action. The test of their leadership growth lay in its effects on student learning.

These travelers were members of the Maine Academy for School Leaders, a professional development program that fused leadership development and school improvement activities in a single model. Traditionally, school leadership training has stood quite apart from school improvement (Milstein & Associates, 1993; Murphy, 1992). School improvement strategies, although they often address the significance of leadership, seldom have tied the development of leadership among both principals and teachers to the success of organizational change (Fullan & Hargreaves, 1991).

The failure of approaches to leadership development and school improvement during the late 1980s and early 1990s led to a number of initiatives to learn anew about how these processes interrelate. The Maine Academy for School Leaders (MASL) was one of five leadership academies funded in 1991 by the U.S. Department of Education. Sponsored by the Maine Leadership Consortium of education institutions and organizations, the Academy's purpose was to try an innovative approach to leadership development, the success of which could be measured by the improvement of children's learning. This feature—linking leadership effectiveness directly to the improvement of student outcomes—was itself a significant innovation in the leadership development field.

Three other major features marked the Maine Academy as innovative. First, MASL defined school leadership as a matter of professional ambition and not as a function of professional position; half of MASL's 58 members were teachers and other nonadministrators. Second, MASL saw leadership development as not merely an intellectual or cognitive process; most important, it posited that leadership cannot grow more effective without behavioral change on the part of the leader as he or she works with other people. Third, the Maine Academy proposed that the primary agent in leadership development was the leader him- or herself; educators applied for membership and were accepted on the understanding that they wanted to find more effective ways to influence others in the day-to-day action and relationships of their schools.

This book explores the soundness of these convictions about leadership development. As staff members of MASL, our curiosity compelled us to write about the impacts of the MASL experiences on both its members and their schools. In one sense, it analyzes members' experiences and asks, "How did the Academy program contribute to—or fail to contribute to—these leaders' growth?" We expect that readers who conduct leadership development programs as consultants, university faculty, and professional associations will find in our book insights into the nature of leadership growth and the structures and processes that can nurture it.

In another and wider sense, however, our book is not about the Academy program but about teachers, principals, teaching principals, and others working to transform their own leadership practices—and thereby their schools. From the developmental stories of these Maine educators, we have expanded our understanding of the variety and richness of leader experiences, and particularly of the meaning those leaders made of them. We expect that teacher leaders, principals, and other school-based leaders will read about many experiences and struggles that parallel their own. We trust that the lessons discovered by our Maine colleagues will help break new ground in others' learning about their own leadership.

We have learned much from practitioners' writing and hope, in the ample quotes we provide, to inspire and elevate the journeys of other front-line leaders. We especially hope that superintendents, school board members, and district staff development committees will find here valuable ways to support, challenge, and sustain growth in school leaders as they go about their everyday activities in schools.

The chapters of our book trace the evolution of MASL members' professional and personal development. Chapter 1 introduces the Academy program and explains how we distilled the experiences of 58 leaders over 16 months to fit the framework of our book. Chapters 2 and 3 address the important preparation stages for professional growth. Chapter 2 reports how MASL members assessed leadership needs in their schools and determined leadership development goals for themselves that might enable them to meet some of these needs. Chapter 3 explores the difficult process of specifying and refining these goals so they can be acted on. It describes how members specified leadership behaviors that they could work on changing in their effort to move their leadership toward the desired goals.

Chapters 4 through 6 are devoted to the processes MASL members used to change their leadership behaviors. Chapter 4 documents what members actually did as they tried to adopt new behaviors in their daily work at school. Chapters 5 and 6 describe the roles and influences of the Support and Development (S&D) Teams and of the MASL facilitators in helping these behavioral changes to succeed.

Chapters 7 and 8 examine the effects or outcomes of these efforts to change, reporting the evaluations of progress by members themselves and by others. Chapter 7 reports the impacts of new leadership behaviors on leaders' schools (an evaluation task that proved very difficult but very powerful when it succeeded). Chapter 8 documents the appreciably easier to retrieve evidence of impacts on the leaders themselves.

In Chapter 9 we reflect on what we, the authors, have learned about the nature of leadership development and the prospects for linking leadership performance to student performance in schools. In our view, leadership growth turns out to be a decidedly unruly process, one that in the cases of our MASL colleagues did not occur in a linear or even cyclic fashion. It is highly individual and often deeply personal; to succeed, it requires a framework for learning and the stalwart companionship of honest professional colleagues, both from within one's school and from without.

For the two of us—a principal and a professor—the Academy and this book have been an unparalleled education. Foremost among our teachers have been the members of the Academy itself. Their courage to risk new leadership behaviors in their schools and to open themselves to new ideas and relationships has truly inspired us. Their continuing willingness to share their experiences with one another has made us all a community of learners. In a partner volume, *As Leaders Learn: Personal Stories of Growth in School Leadership* (Corwin, 1995), nine Academy members describe their continuing learning-in-action as school leaders.

We have learned as well from many "colleague-critics." Sue Martin and Dick Barnes, our fellow MASL staff members, hold a special place in our pantheon of teachers and friends. Others whose feedback on this manuscript made it more comprehensible both to us and, we think, to readers include Roland Barth, Gary Whiteley, David Hagstrom, Becky van der Bogert, Judy Lucarelli, Bob Wimpelberg, Dave Brown, and Dave Erlandson. Special thanks must go to Nelson Walls of the Maine Leadership Consortium who helped make MASL possible; to the College of Education of the University of Maine for their continued support; and to Linda Syphers who persisted through many "final" drafts of this book.

A deep sense of love and appreciation are due Margarita, Anna and Isaac and Cynthia, Morgaen, Cary, Nell, and Ben for their understanding, support, and gift of time as we roamed the state for Academy events and cut into family time to finish this book.

We cannot predict all the lessons our readers will glean from our book and its pioneers. Indeed, by richly sampling these leaders' words in the following pages, we have tried to make their experiences directly accessible to our readers so that, in the spirit of the Academy, our readers can make their own sense of the journey toward better leadership.

GORDON A. DONALDSON JR.
GEORGE F. MARNIK

# ABOUT THE AUTHORS

**Gordon A. Donaldson Jr.** has written about school leadership and has helped create new leadership development opportunities since the mid-1970s. He was a cofounder of the Maine Principals' Academy, a founding member of the International Network of Principals' Centers, and served as director of the Maine Academy for School Leaders. He has taught in Pennsylvania, Massachusetts, and Maine, where he was also a principal. He is author of *Learning to Lead: The Dynamics of the High School Principalship* (Greenwood, 1991). He holds degrees from Harvard College and the Harvard Graduate School of Education, Cambridge, MA, and is currently Professor of Education at the University of Maine. He lives in Lamoine, Maine, with his family and several derelict boats.

**George F. Marnik** worked as one of the two facilitators for the Maine Academy for School Leaders. During this time he was on leave of absence from Deer Isle-Stonington Junior/Senior High School, where he taught and had been a principal for 12 years. After funding for the Academy expired, he returned to his school district on a part-time basis—as Assistant Principal for its two elementary schools and as K-12 Staff and Curriculum Development

Coordinator. This part-time arrangement has given him the freedom to complete his doctoral course work in Educational Leadership at the University of Maine. He also helps coordinate statewide efforts to nurture the ever-expanding Maine Network of School Leaders. Prior to his work in Maine, he taught in Philadelphia while attending graduate school and earned an M.Ed. from Temple University in 1972. For several years in both Philadelphia and Camden, New Jersey, he was actively involved in developing and directing alternative education programs for students disenfranchised from traditional middle and high school programs.

# THE CHALLENGE
## Improve Schools
## Through Improving Leadership

The horizon leans forward,
Offering you space
To place new steps of change
Here, on the pulse of this fine day
You may have the courage
To look up and out and upon me . . .

Maya Angelou, *On the Pulse of Morning* (1993)

**S**ix educators sat huddled in a conference room in May 1993, conversing intently. The topic was leadership—how their own leadership was going in their schools. Ed, an elementary teaching principal, was describing a breakthrough for himself: "I couldn't understand why I was feeling like such a failure, why I'd have done just about anything to get out of [my position]. I thought it was that I was too much of an autocrat, not enough of a democrat, so I was trying to give teachers more say. In fact, it was that I wasn't hearing the faculty say, 'No, that's not it! It's that you can't delegate. You feel you must do it all yourself.' I feel so much better—and I think I've *been* a better principal—since I've been working on controlling that need in myself."

Becky, a secondary guidance counselor chimed in: "I felt I was running all over the place trying to influence everything at once, but failing to make much of a dent at all. I needed to focus, to find a goal.

1

In my Leadership Development Plan, I kept asking, 'Of all the many things I do, what is the key? Where can I make the biggest impact for kids in my school?' I found that by acknowledging people and their ideas more, I no longer feel I need to do it all . . . I've got to seek others out and *share* the joy and the responsibility of changing our school. As I have tried to be more collaborative in my work with my principal and teachers, I'm feeling more focused, less frantic, and more influential for kids."

Ed's eagerness to piggyback on Becky's point was palpable: "Yes! That's what I found, even though it was very difficult for me. Plans that are made in isolation don't really go anyplace. That was a real revelation for me. . . . In recent months, I've been trying to give the staff what *they say* they need rather than what *I think* they need!"

Becky, Ed, and their colleagues spent 3 hours sharing lessons from their 16-month efforts to transform their leadership. These were their exhibitions to one another of the lessons they had learned from trying to influence their schools to improve student learning. It was the culmination of many months of effort at becoming better leaders. The lessons reflected the ups and downs and the often deeply personal nature of leadership growth.

Nancy, a teacher leader, depicted her development through a series of photographs representing the evolution of her vision as a leader. As her commentary moved from picture to picture, she became more personal in her reflections: "This is really about me and how I didn't see myself as a leader even though I was in leadership positions [as team leader and association president]. What I've been able to do this year is create for myself a self-concept as a leader. . . . I now see how I am influencing others for the good of the kids and I'm in better control of it."

And Tess, also a teacher leader, presented her learning by show-ing a videotape of herself facilitating a curriculum committee at her school. As the group watched the tape, Tess provided a voice-over: "Here we're trying to make a decision. I didn't want to push too hard for my position just now. It was really important that these people hear what the consultant was saying and get a chance to evaluate her input. But I was trying to make sure that everyone was saying what was on their minds, so we didn't have a small group who might circle their wagons outside the meeting." As she talked, Tess compared her behaviors on the tape to behaviors she would have used 16 months before.

In other rooms of the Sugarloaf U.S.A. conference center, other groups of school leaders were having similar conversations. They were the 58 members of the Maine Academy for School Leaders (MASL), a federally funded innovative leadership development program created by the Maine Leadership Consortium. In February 1992, they had begun the Academy as a collection of mostly teachers and principals seeking to become more positive schoolwide influences for student learning in their schools. Now, as the Academy program was ending, they reflected on how their daily work at school had changed—or had not changed—and shared the evidence that these changes had—or had not—influenced the learning of students.

This book is about these 58 leaders and their journeys toward greater schoolwide influence. It is a collage of leadership growth experiences as told primarily by these Maine leaders themselves. Their journeys were neither easy nor straight. As Becky put it, "I learned that the things you learn aren't always in the places you think you'll learn them." Becoming a better school leader, we found, took great energy, courage, patience, and collegial support. But the rewards, on both personal and professional scales, often surpassed the emotional, intellectual, and practical investments.

The stories here are all about leaders who, in Maya Angelou's words, tried to make the "horizon lean forward" to "offer space to place new steps of change" for themselves and their schools. Their personal accounts of change, we hope, will guide the future work of leadership development programs and staff development for principals and teachers. For principals and teachers everywhere working to make their schools better, these Maine leaders' stories will, we trust, both enlighten and inspire.

## The Maine Academy Model

Although our book focuses primarily on the leaders and their efforts to grow, the Academy program structured the context for those efforts. This section describes the philosophy and structure of that program. The model for the Academy rested on three cornerstone principles:

*Principle 1: True school leaders enhance learning outcomes for students through influencing others in the school community to*

*take collaborative responsibility and action for their own learn-
ing and work.*

Although the cause-and-effect relationship between a leader's
behavior and a student's learning is often extremely difficult to
identify, much less influence, Academy activities required members
to define their development in terms of potential student gains. This
meant viewing leadership as a matter of influencing other adults
who were directly teaching, counseling, coaching, and raising children. Drawing on the work of Barth (1991), Levine (1989), and
Sergiovanni (1992), among others, we encouraged members to understand their leadership effects on student learning *as mediated by
their relationships with adults.* As we shall see, the work of leadership
improvement often centered on the challenge of influencing colleagues and parents while maintaining an open, collaborative relationship with them.

> *Principle 2: Learning to lead more effectively involves learning
> how one's beliefs and behaviors at school affect others and, in
> turn, how this cumulatively influences how well students
> learn.*

The Academy structured members' learning to focus on their
behaviors as well as their beliefs. We took this tack on the premise
that one educator's influence on another or on a parent is more
strongly affected by what that educator *does* than what he or she *says*
(Argyris & Schön, 1974; Fullan & Hargreaves, 1991; Lieberman,
1988). Academy activities pushed members to examine how their
behaviors with and toward their colleagues—those they hoped to
lead—built trust, open inquiry, collegial teamwork, and encouragement for trying new behaviors with children.

As the Academy proceeded, we came to understand leadership
growth as a three-dimensional process: It requires changes in the
leader's thinking (cognitive domain) and behaviors with others
(interpersonal domain); but these do not readily occur without
significant self-examination and self-change (intrapersonal domain).
As documents in the Appendix indicate, many of the Academy's
sessions and activities revolved around work in these three domains
and they became known under the rubric of the Interpersonal-
Cognitive-Intrapersonal (I-C-I) model. The work of Howard Gardner

(1993) and Donald Schön (1983) guided our thinking toward this model (Donaldson, 1993).

> *Principle 3: School leaders learn best when they fashion their own goals and follow their own learning styles, but they also need a supportive, colleague-critic network that is committed to such learning-in-action.*

The third principle echoes the essence of adult learning or androgogy (Knowles, 1984) and asserts that school leaders become more effective when they publicly model learning for their school communities. We structured most of the Academy's activities to give members the responsibility to determine the need for their own learning and the liberty to pursue that learning in their own style and manner (Little, 1986; Osterman & Kottkamp, 1993). But we also structured the experience to surround each member with trusted and supportive colleague-critics and to create among us a "community of learners" (Barth, 1991).

The Academy required each member to develop a Leadership Development Plan (LDP) tailored to his or her own school's leadership needs and his or her own personality and goals. Members identified in these plans strategies for improving in their daily work at school. Then, through two full-time facilitators and a colleague-critic team for each member, we attempted to provide continuous emotional support, observational feedback on progress, and technical resources while our members worked to change their behaviors in the action of their schools.

These principles drove Academy activities in several unusual ways. They focused each leader's learning on his or her own behavior, knowledge, and skills. Learning needs were derived from the "fit" of these with the improvement needs of his or her own school. Hence learning revolved around in-school issues and experiences, not around theory or generalized knowledge presented by the Academy. Academy sessions presented opportunities to prepare for new in-action behaviors at school. The two full-time Academy facilitators "rode circuit" among members' schools to consult regularly with each member and to meet with each colleague-critic team, known as a Support and Development (S&D) Team.

The program sketch in Figure 1.1 summarizes the four phases of the 16-month Academy program. Note that, as well as meeting in

**Maine Academy for School Leaders**

| | Major Goals | Structure | MASL Documents to Reference* |
|---|---|---|---|
| Phase I | **Assessing My Leadership**<br>Evaluate leadership strengths/needs of<br>School program<br>Staff context<br>Self<br><br>Begin Leadership Development Plan (LDP)<br>Network/group formation | **February-June**<br>Biweekly sessions in network (30) or regional group (15)<br>Led by staff | "The Leadership Development Plan"<br>"Examining My Leadership"<br>"LDP Criteria" |
| Phase II | **The Leadership Development Plan**<br>Seek resources to prepare and refine LDP<br>Form Support and Development (S&D) Team (3-4)<br>Skills awareness sessions/simulations<br>Create entry plans | **June-August**<br>Three network/group sessions<br>6-day residential institute led by staff, resource people<br>Staff and colleague feedback<br>S&D Teams become active | Support & Development Team Goals<br>"MASL Summer Institute"<br>"LDP Synopsis"<br>"Entry Plan"<br>"S&D Team Agreement" |

*See Donaldson, Mainik, Martin, and Barnes (1993).

6

**Phase III** **Changing My Behaviors**

| | August-May | |
|---|---|---|
| Pursue LDP in workplace; modify leader behavior—evaluate—reformulate | Workplace-centered | "Talking With Colleagues About My Practice" |
| | S&D Teams meet/observe and feedback | "Taking Stock" |
| Specific "training" or resource assistance to fit LDP needs | Facilitators work 1 to 1, with S&Ds, as network web-weavers | "Evaluating Our S&D Team" |
| Strengthen functioning of S&D teams as colleague-critic | Shoot for weekly contact | |
| | Monthly network/ Academy gatherings | |
| | Increasing member control over program | |

**Phase IV** **Exhibiting Leadership Learning**

| | April-June | |
|---|---|---|
| Document Phase I-II efforts | Reflective practice | "Assessing Leadership Improvement: Building and Using a Leadership Portfolio" |
| Collect feedback to evaluate growth | Behavioral feedback from workplace/MASL | "Evaluating Our Leadership Portfolio" |
| Prepare portfolio | Journals and documents exhibit changes in leadership (I-C-I) | |
| Present exhibition of leadership learning | | |

**Figure 1.1.** The Maine Academy for School Leaders: A Program Sketch

S&D Teams, members gathered as a whole group of 58 approximately every 8 to 12 weeks and as network groups of 30 or regional groups of 15 approximately every 3 to 4 weeks. These sessions were devoted initially to establishing the Academy curriculum framework but, as LDPs were established, they were increasingly used to connect members with resources and training *in response* to the learning needs identified in their Leadership Development Plans and in S&D Team meetings. A *Curriculum Packet*, published by the Maine Leadership Consortium (Donaldson, Marnik, Martin, & Barnes, 1993), describes the program more fully.

Members evaluated their growth through regular reflective journaling, periodic "taking stock" activities based on their LDP, and a portfolio and exhibition of learning in May 1993. An independent evaluation of MASL (Johnson, Morris, & Nicoletti, 1993) concluded that "participants have been significantly changed as a result of their participation in the Academy. . . . [They] have changed in a way that will continue to have an impact on their leadership behavior in schools" (p. 73). With the termination of federal funding in June 1993, Academy members formed the Maine Network of School Leaders to encourage ongoing support for leadership development for themselves and for an expanding community of school leaders in Maine.

## Capturing Leaders'
## Learning in Their Own Words

We regard the members of the Maine Academy as pioneers in two important ways. As a group, MASL's 58 members and four staff members explored in action our three cornerstone principles. In collecting and analyzing members' experiences for this book, we looked for commonalities among them to see if and how each principle held up.

But, individual by individual, these members were pioneers as well because each member was expected to make discernible changes in his or her professional behavior to improve his or her school. In accepting responsibility for changing their own behaviors, these leaders faced the unsettling fallout from shifting established relationships with others at work and altering secure and well-worn patterns of activity at work. MASL challenged them to use the reflections they saw in the professional mirrors held up to them by

MASL colleagues, colleagues at work, and ultimately by themselves to set new courses for themselves and their schools.

Neither the collective journey nor the individual journeys can be cleanly sequenced or neatly packaged. Quite to the contrary, they were full of dense underbrush, dead ends, and uncertain directions and destinations. For these Maine educators, the journey stopped and started many times as the demands of "simply doing my job" made "work on doing it better" extremely difficult. Doubt plagued most throughout—about their capacity to lead, about the possibility of ever "really" influencing the learning of students, about their personal right to influence others, about their stamina to see it all through.

We have attempted to capture critical developmental events in the individual and collective journeys of these adventurous souls. We have organized our retelling of their experiences chronologically to show common developmental challenges and turning points. Our sources were the ample writings of MASL members collected over the life of the Academy. These included original applications to MASL, journal entries, drafts of LDPs, periodic "taking stock" self-assessments of progress, feedback collected from colleagues, the final Leadership Portfolios, and staff field notes. Illustrations of our observations come, with member permission, from the words of MASL leaders found in these rich documents (members are identified by pseudonyms).

Space limitations have forced us to simplify these developmental journeys, omitting details and variations in favor of identifying commonalities. We have underrepresented the frustrations many felt in order to display the "ahas" and leaps forward. Similarly, we have largely omitted discussion of a half dozen members who, to the best of our knowledge, made only meager progress. We would have, as well, liked to explore all the differences between teacher leaders' journeys and principals' journeys. In exchange for these limitations, we believe that we have richly illustrated the modal experience of those who made significant strides toward improving their effectiveness as leaders in their own schools.

More often than not, these teachers and principals articulated their own learning in colorful and passionate terms. Our task was not so much to decide what members had learned about their leadership as it was to choose among all the "learnings" our members wrote about. They were prolific in their writing and, as the Academy went on, their abilities to recount and evaluate what they learned became eminently more sophisticated.

A letter we received a month after the Academy ended illustrates this point and provides a fitting conclusion to this introduction. Fran wrote to us and to her S&D Team on June 15, 1993, the last "student day" in her first year as a middle school principal:

Dear Laura, Shelly, Alex, George, and Gordie:

As I looked over 509 students this morning and said good-bye to my eighth graders, I felt a knot in my stomach and a lump in my throat. Later, I waved good-bye to everyone and walked back through some very empty halls and thought about the events of the last 10 months. I had an overwhelming feeling of gratefulness that you were all a very important part of it.

We celebrated today, and it felt good. The end of the year was remarkably quiet, and the morale among the adults remained high. As you know, it wasn't always like that here, especially this past winter. Then, after spring vacation, we started to have some conversations about how the attitude and behaviors of the adults are reflected in the children. Therefore, if we were going to make it, we needed to pull together and set a more positive tone. We did. I am finishing the year with an incredible feeling of pride in what we have accomplished, survived, and overcome. Deep down inside, I am fully aware that without the experience of the Academy and your constant support, I would never have gained the skills, thought processes, and insight that guided me through this year.

The Academy introduced me to the "professional" me. With your support I was able to face my weaknesses and find a way to improve in those areas. I learned to plan and carry out plans that allowed me more time with students, parents, and staff. I rarely fell into the "putting out the brush fire" mode, and was able to deal with daily events in a calm (OK, usually calm) manner that avoided adding more chaos to crisis. Throughout the year, I learned to use strategies and plan my reactions whenever possible, especially during some of those stressful conversations principals must have.

I thought more than I ever have about the job we do as educators and the job I do as a school leader. And the thoughts continue. I have learned to believe in myself and find myself forming an identity—not as someone's daughter, sister, or wife, but of me and who I am as a leader. I find myself still reading a great deal, and constantly thinking about how we can be better. . . .

I have started to work on my next LDP—planning for next year, assessing my first year, and looking at areas that need some attention. My S&D Team will be very happy to know that I am taking a look at my "personal" side of my professional me!! I have realized that you were right: My taking care of everyone else and being reluctant to let anyone take care of me is not always healthy, smart, or good. Over the past few weeks I have attempted to open up and lean on some people.

Perhaps this year drove me to the point where I needed to make sure that everything is all right because I was terribly afraid of failing. If we failed, it would be because I was (OK, multiple choice:) young, inexperienced, or a woman. Feeling more secure about myself in this position has allowed me to "loosen" up and turn to others for support. I remember Alex so strongly asking me at Fairview Elementary what I was doing for myself, not just for the school, the kids, the teachers. Well I may be slow, but I have started to think about it, and plan on acting on it.

Although I know that you are all out there, I miss us and the Academy. I don't think you realize how much support you were to me this year, or how much I learned from all of you. I guess the old saying that you don't miss something until it's gone is true. . . . I know I have so much to learn . . . but where, from whom, and how seem to be recurring concerns [now that the Academy has ended].

Take care!!!

Fran

# FINDING A STARTING PLACE
# FOR LEADERSHIP GROWTH

> Rather than thinking only in terms of what changes I should try
> to bring about, . . . I have begun to think in terms of how my
> feelings, behaviors, and reactions to how others act toward me
> might lessen my effectiveness. . . . I think I need a sharp focus
> on the real.
>
> *Orin* 6/92

The 58 members of the Maine Academy for School Leaders began
their leadership development work with a single lofty goal: To
improve their leadership so that student learning outcomes would
improve in their schools in some perceptible way. The MASL program and staff set this forth as a nonnegotiable. We knew from the
outset that this was likely to be an extraordinarily difficult goal to meet
in 16 months. We did not realize, however, how challenging our
members would find it simply to define a starting place to begin from.

This chapter describes Academy members' initial efforts to ex-
pand leadership capacities. These first activities dwelled on framing
a basic understanding of school leadership and professional growth.
They carried members from exploring how well their schools served
students to pinning down how their own behaviors might change
to lead their schools to do better. For most, these initial steps in the
journey to leadership growth proved challenging, unsettling, and
exhilarating.

Phase I of the Academy, from February 1991 through June 1992, was designed to help members do three things: (a) assess their schools' performance with students, (b) derive from those assessments some leadership challenges, and (c) build their own developmental goals around these challenges. Members talked with colleagues at work, pawed through documentary evidence of student performance, listened to other MASL members' assessments, and thought a great deal about how their practice as leaders could be enhanced in demonstrable ways. The Academy also expected all members to come to its summer institute in July with an assessment of their school and themselves that would be a foundation for a Leadership Development Plan spelling out developmental goals for themselves linked to student outcomes for the school.

This chapter describes MASL members' common experiences as they moved through this initial assessment and goal-finding process. For most, it was a process that began easily enough with the needs of their schools' students. But as they began addressing how they might influence their schools to improve student performance, many members encountered a fog bank of personal, interpersonal, and school culture issues. Their ability to navigate in this fog bank and to emerge with useful leadership growth goals proved extraordinarily important to their eventual success in the Academy.

## A Clear Start:
## What Our Students Need

In February, each leader was asked to identify student learning challenges his or her school faced. Staff encouraged members to write about these in summary descriptions and collect documentation to anchor these student outcome goals in real data. Then, in March, Academy activities began to focus on the leadership challenges inherent in moving members' schools toward addressing some of these student needs.

The first of these two steps, identifying student outcome goals, proved relatively straightforward, but the second, assessing how to affect them, did not. When members examined their schools' success with students, they had no problem listing which student outcomes needed improvement: achievement scores, comfort with computers as learning tools, respecting their peers, developing cooperative work skills, addressing the needs of at-risk students—the lists were ready-made and long. MASL leaders' major challenge was not coming up with a list but identifying one or two of these student outcomes that they could reasonably expect to affect. It was not uncommon in the early Academy meetings to hear members—and especially the teacher leaders in the group—ask, "How am I going to do all this?"

Indeed, the brave goal of changing student outcomes intimidated nearly everyone. Looking back, we now realize that most members skirted this impossible goal by sensibly turning their attention to specific programs associated with one or two student outcome goals. That is, few members dwelt extensively on understanding the problems of student learning in their schools; they jumped rapidly to shaping existing structures and solutions. For example, Irene, a junior high principal, framed her early "student outcome" goal as "the improvement of discipline procedures/techniques for students at Stevens School" (*Irene* 3/92).

Most Academy members whittled down their laundry lists of student outcomes by focusing not on the student outcome but on the *school activity* that they assumed addressed that set of outcomes. Thus a concern for student achievement quickly refocused for one member on ways to build parent involvement; improving mathematics learning shifted to implementing the new National Council of Teachers of Mathematics (NCTM) outcome standards; similarly, improved abilities for self-expression became developing a writing lab; enhancing children's multiple modes of learning became using authentic assessment strategies; meeting the needs of at-risk kids turned into developing alternative programs for at-risk students. These programmatic improvement goals were, in one sense, easy to come up with: Members' schools buzzed with ideas such as these, and school reform literature and professional journals offered more than enough new programs. Framing their goals in terms of shaping programs made them feel more attainable and concrete.

In the opening months of the Academy, then, most members worked diligently at two things: (a) creating descriptions of student needs, and then (b) framing their leadership ambitions in terms of acting on programs that presumably would address some of these needs. This brought the typical Maine leader face to face with a new challenge: describing just *how* these programs were going to change student learning for the better. MASL members felt two competing forces as they pushed beyond *what* to change and began considering *how* they were going to change it. On one hand, their school assessment activities made clear some steps for enacting program innovations they believed would lead to specific student outcomes. These steps were often articulated as prescriptions for their schools. On the other hand, however, few members felt comfortable prescribing changes to their staffs and colleagues. The "how to" challenge, as we shall see in the next section, brought members face to face with a set of interpersonal dilemmas.

Carl, an elementary principal, provided a good example of the initial tendency to construct leadership plans that were implicitly prescriptive. He planned to improve school climate by following these steps:

1. Establish a steering committee . . .
2. Collect baseline data
3. Conduct awareness-raising activities so that parents, students, and staff are informed . . .
4. Conduct an assessment of the school's climate
5. Identify improvement priorities and develop action plans . . .
6. Organize task forces to accomplish the tasks . . .
7. Coordinate the work of the task forces
8. Evaluate the overall impact . . . (*Carl* 6/92)

Typical of many members' early leadership plans, these eight steps describe *activities* that needed to be done, not strategies for getting them done. In the effort to delineate leadership goals, most MASL colleagues moved first to such relatively tidy lists of what they and others needed to accomplish. Beyond this step, however, lay the vital and considerably messier details of the interpersonal negotiations, relationships, and dynamics that would move them, their colleagues, students, and parents actually to *do* these activities.

## If I Lead, Will They Follow?

As members increasingly encountered the sticky "how to" challenge, Academy sessions engaged them in exploring three questions in an activity titled "Examining My Leadership" (see the Appendix):

1. What is my ideal/model leader like?

2. How do the relationships among people in my school help or hinder my leadership?

3. What capabilities do I have that will enable me to succeed as a leader for my school?

Between March and July, members undertook a number of activities designed to assist in their self-assessment around these three questions (such as the Myers-Briggs Type Indicator and the Conflict Management Style Inventory, a series of leadership role-plays, and extensive discussion, reflection, and writing sessions). The flow of this new information tended to make the picture of their leadership increasingly complex. This was unsettling for many, but at the same time it felt, as one teacher leader put it, "refreshingly real" in contrast to the remoteness of prescribed plans.

"Examining My Leadership" and the Academy's emphasis on exploring interpersonal dynamics through role-plays forced members to face the challenges of motivating, collaborating with, and shaping the behaviors of adults in their schools to reach their goals for students. The vast majority of members emerged from this work with three realizations: (a) they philosophically opposed a leadership approach in which they would tell staff or colleagues what they needed to do, (b) research on school change indicated that such an approach often does not work, and (c) they did not directly or indirectly control either the staff or the students to a sufficient degree to make their own prescriptions work. They could not unilaterally make changes in their schools, no matter how right their solutions might be.

Typically, this led members to grapple with another conception of the "how to" leadership challenge: Leading school change meant having other adults change *their* behaviors, attitudes, beliefs, and practices. Their diagnoses of school needs thus made Academy members face the question: What gives me the right to ask a colleague to change? Many members, and especially the teachers in the group, knew how they would make changes in their own classrooms, but the Academy was asking them to consider affecting such changes in others' classrooms, in hallways, athletic fields, and school buses.

With this realization, members' leadership development took on another layer of complexity: To the task of linking student outcomes to programmatic changes they now added changing staff relationships and performance. Chauncey, a high school assistant principal, illustrates this connection. He at first identified at-risk student outcomes as a pressing need for his school and thus for his leadership development focus. In the process of assessing how the school might improve its work with at-risk kids, he explored ways the school's alternative education program worked and what his role in it was. He wrote as part of his initial "Examining My Leadership" about his various roles:

>    1. As assistant principal and student assistance team member I directly intervene with "at-risk" students. Interventions include. . . .
>    2. As supervisor, I oversee the alternative educational referral process and programs and special education as well. I am responsible for these systems' effectiveness. As an evaluator, I am responsible for the effectiveness of the staff members who work in those areas. . . .
>    3. As supervisor-evaluator for the science cluster, I influence the curriculum and the quality of instruction, which indirectly affects students learning in this area.
>    4. As facilitator for the school improvement team, I influence the effectiveness of the team itself, which is the formal body responsible for promoting improvements in learning and teaching. . . . (*Chauncey* 3/92)

In subsequent MASL activities and discussions, Chauncey came to understand that the process of leading change would involve him in the intricate web of "people needs" throughout Ellington High. By July, he saw his leadership challenge as "changing norms and beliefs" among staff, a far cry from simply reformulating the alternative education program:

> People needs at Ellington must be addressed in order to promote success with the at-risk student population. It has been normative at Ellington to focus on problems (i.e., what is *not* working). There has been a prevailing belief that initiatives and innovations "will never fly." When challenges arise that require collaboration, as most do, it is normal for individuals and groups to avoid solutions that require more than a few close

colleagues to collaborate. It is normal to focus on barriers and to avoid processes that generate solutions. . . .

Given the picture above, it is necessary to change norms and certain beliefs among those individuals and groups dedicated to working with not only at-risk but all students. . . . Promoting the values and activities of collaboration is vital for an effective system. . . . (*Chauncey* 7/92)

Most Academy members traveled Chancey's path from identifying student needs to eventually restating their goals in terms of making staff change. Academy activities and the "Examining My Leadership" structure encouraged this trek. For most, it came as a mixed blessing. On one hand, it gave their planning a realism and immediacy that they found heartening; they intuitively knew that real change in student learning needed to involve staff change. On the other hand, leading adults to think, act, and even believe differently in themselves and their work was a daunting and unknown process for most, especially in the collaborative mode the Academy encouraged. Karen, an elementary teacher leader, for example, expressed fear and trepidation at the following newly conceived leadership challenge:

In my school there is a largely senior staff that is highly competent and quite proud of their accomplishments and the school's reputation. . . . Among this group of professionals I frequently see entrenchment. The attitudes "I've seen this before, I don't need this. . . . I've done fine for 25 years without this. . . . If it ain't broke, don't fix it" are frequently voiced. (*Karen* 4/92)

After a fast start identifying what students needed and what program changes could help them, members found themselves entering a fog as they struggled to determine *how* to lead these changes.

## Navigating From Ideal to Real

Over the first months of the Academy, most members' aspirations for changing student learning gradually became tempered by realities in their schools. With time, support, and the Academy's relentless emphasis on making their leadership growth "make a difference at school," members could not easily maintain an unrealistically orderly image of their work. Their leadership tasks simply boiled with too many unknowns: varieties of students and staff, philosophies and curriculum options, political and logistical factors, personal and interpersonal issues.

This proved unsettling for most, as it meant pushing the limits of their understanding into new frontiers. In contrast to the crisp black-and-white world of textbooks and restructuring plans and their earlier idealized goals for student outcomes, MASL leaders struggled with the ungainly interpersonal mysteries of how to influence their colleagues to want to change. This challenge introduced what one member called "this gray stuff":

> I felt a vacuum yesterday [when we were working to define our leadership development goals] . . . but now I see that that was to my benefit. . . . If I had been clearer about what I was going to do to improve how I lead, I wouldn't have come up with my own agenda. . . . This gray stuff is new . . . and I'm starting to like it. . . . I've learned more about myself as a leader in the last 2 months than in my whole graduate program. (*Fran* 3/92)

Struggling with the "gray stuff" of influencing others while maintaining interpersonal relationships helped many members like Fran to tailor their own agendas for themselves to grow as leaders. The creation of these agendas proved an essential step in the developmental process for many.

How did that work for most? It seems to have involved two shifts in thought and attitude: (a) taming their visions of the ideal leader and (b) coming to grips with some realities about themselves as "influencers" of their colleagues at school. Altogether, the hard work of making these discoveries palpably energized many of the group, giving them confidence and direction as growing leaders.

The first of these shifts—the challenge of taming their visions of the ideal—took a lot of time, discussion, and support from colleagues. For many, it began with articulating those ideals, something the "Examining My Leadership" framework structured and encouraged over the initial months. Confronted with their own ambitious goals for changing student learning outcomes, most members suffered setbacks to their confidence as they contemplated various images of "super leaders." Typical was this principal's overwhelming

concept of what she expected of herself and what her community
wanted in a leader:

What is my ideal/model leader like?
- Charismatic, trust builder, has vision, high work ethic,
  goes the extra mile, pleasant, upbeat, able to make decisions, caring, intelligent and articulate, good problem
  solver but able to lead others to problem solve also,
  patient, intuitive, good time manager

What does my school and community expect in a leader? What
    do they need?
- All of the above, plus . . . a person who can set and attain
  goals built around a vision. This vision must be articulated and "bought" by both the school and community
  at large.

What capabilities do I have/not have that will enable me to
    succeed as a leader in my school?
- I hope I have all or most of the above. . . .

What component of leadership are you most challenged and
    intrigued by?
- Keeping all of the above qualities going simultaneously
  while "stretching" to add new programs, students, space,
  staff without losing quality. (*Kelly* 4/92)

Idealistic expectations of this sort came from current literature
and popular conceptions of the effective leader, from members'
experiences with revered principals and colleagues, and, especially
for the teacher leaders, from their negative experiences with current
or past administrators. To a person, MASL members envisioned a
leader who was more compassionate, collaborative, respectful of
diversity, and involved with teaching and learning than the traditional school manager or executive (Jerry Murphy's 1988 depiction
of "heroic" and "unheroic" leaders was a favorite reading for many).
A secondary school teacher leader typified the ease with which
many identified what they did *not* want to be:

My school is full of strong, dedicated, bright, and caring teachers. Their central focus is the kids. We take the word "administrator" literally; we want a leader who'll minister to our needs. Because we are a strong and diverse group, we serve well an equally diverse student population. Our strength demands a strong leader. We don't have one.

Our administrator's style is not well matched to the community ethic which has driven our school. He lacks both personal and professional confidence. He does not like to work in groups larger than five, but has not reorganized our traditional structure. He admittedly "does not read." When observing a class where I was facilitating cooperative learning, he asked if he could come back sometime when I was "really teaching."

This "leadership" has created an atmosphere of every man for himself; any positive action or innovation is perceived by him and by some faculty, now, as self-serving. (*Barbara* 5/92)

Membership in MASL and discussions among members at sessions sometimes heightened expectations for "super leadership" by coalescing feeling against traditional practices of this kind. But Academy activities and staff invited members to "tame their ideals" by constantly challenging them to identify concrete opportunities in their schools to behave more like their ideals and cautioning that changes in their own behaviors would not happen overnight. Like the cold moist air meeting the hot clear air, the mixing of school realities with ideal visions was responsible for the "gray fog" through which many members moved. Navigating through this fog seemed to require both recognizing that they could not instantly become ideal leaders and locating some realistic place to start working. One middle school teacher leader said it very nicely:

I think we're dealing with at least two levels, the ideal and the practical. The goal should be for current school leaders to look to the models we've studied/practiced as a goal toward which they are actively moving. . . . HOPEFULLY, that will occur. . . . I fully see leadership as a journey taken on an internal landscape before it is practiced in the "real" world. I hope this is the case, and that the practical and the ideal will begin to merge. (*Charlotte* 6/92)

This "journey on an internal landscape" involved extensive discussion, thought, sharing with colleagues, and the writing of drafts of leadership development goals. Breakthroughs seemed to come when members discovered that some aspect of their leadership ideal was flawed, that they had made improper assumptions about what or who a leader was. Shelly, a teacher leader, articulated one of her breakthroughs this way:

> One of the most important [ways my thinking about school leadership has changed] is in the area of how school leaders are identified. I always had the notion that leaders had to be officially "appointed," "labeled," and "designated," or otherwise identified by those in authority to have any power to affect change. . . . Now I empower myself, I don't need to be allowed leadership roles. (*Shelly* 6/1)

Breaking out of a prior assumption about leadership empowered Shelly to redefine leadership for both her own situation and herself.

For many members, the taming of ideals was one of the first significant discoveries of the Academy experience, a first "aha." This unfreezing from previous roles and ideals freed them to address realities both within themselves and between themselves and colleagues. In June 1992, Nina described in her journal this meeting of the real and the ideal:

> Prior to the Academy, I spent precious little time thinking about leadership, but rather how change ought to happen. I have learned to connect the two notions. . . . I have learned that leadership has an intrapersonal dimension—something that causes me great angst (Am I the best judge of my own character and beliefs?). . . . I have become far more introspective about understanding and evaluating my own leadership skills in conjunction with my day-to-day work. I am learning to act more and react less, and I am learning to see myself in a leadership role—as an agent for change—influencing the thinking of some members of the group. . . . (*Nina* 6/1)

Taming ideals meant accepting the fact that we cannot become ideal leaders quickly or easily, no matter how much our schools might need to achieve that ideal image. Nina, for example, moved from concentrating on "how change ought to happen" to concentrating on "understanding and evaluating my own leadership skills." This realization seemed to permit members to make the second shift necessary for setting useful goals for themselves: coming to grips with some realities about themselves as influencers of their colleagues at school. With few exceptions, this shift resulted from making observations about their behaviors with others, both in the Academy and at school. Doreen, an elementary teaching principal described in a June 1992 journal entry her changed thinking about how she should be behaving at school:

> The major impact of the Academy thus far is that I am thinking about leadership as an entity unto itself. . . . Now I am ready to learn about . . . how it affects me. The more I read, and the more role-considering we do, the more I realize that perhaps I don't need to be "Oil-Can Doreen," the mechanic who assesses the problem, looks at the possible tools to make the thing work, and then fixes it. (*Doreen* 6/92)

MASL activities were designed largely to encourage this process of "role-considering" or, as another person put it, "finding myself as a leader." From the start, MASL staff structured activities to focus members' attention on the *behaviors* of leadership, to have members look at their own "leading behaviors" with others. Members role-played in simulated school leadership situations and then discussed and reflected on the behaviors used and their effectiveness.

As members pondered the often yawning chasms between espoused theories of leadership and in-action leadership behaviors, they discovered specific behaviors that needed to be changed. Members were encouraged to analyze specific leadership situations they found themselves in at school and to write journal entries evaluating how specific things they did succeeded or failed. MASL offered self-assessment instruments that supplied new vocabularies for self-description and goal-setting (e.g., the Myers-Briggs Type Indicator, the Conflict Management Style Inventory). Later in the Academy, facilitators and S&D Team members observed members at work in their schools and provided direct observational feedback and consultation in this regard. Throughout, the I-C-I model suggested to members that leadership was "not just a matter of having the right ideas" (cognitive domain) but also a matter of behaving with others in productive working relationships (interpersonal domain) and monitoring those behaviors through accurate self-knowledge (intrapersonal domain).

It was this somewhat relentless focus on behaviors and on one's self-knowledge, reinforced by MASL activities that put real behaviors before the group, that led many members to move past "theory" to their immediate realities. A first-year principal wrote in June, 1992:

> I am not so sure that my understanding of leadership has changed as much as the understanding of myself as a leader has changed . . . reflecting, reading, becoming more aware of my weaknesses (such as body language, facial expressions, and severe lack of organization) and have started to direct my strengths into a more focused arena. . . . I guess I would have to say that the feedback that I have received from colleagues in the Academy has been the most useful information I have received. (*Fran* 6/1)

A high school department chairperson attributed her new ability to understand leadership situations to the Academy's interactive activities and the I-C-I model:

> Learning about my own leadership increases when I work with other people. Role-playing (even though I am a reticent participant) was very beneficial in helping me, for I was forced to move from thinking to acting. An issue that appeared to me crystalline on the cognitive level often became cloudy when the dimension of interpersonal dynamics was added. Group discussion and triads were valuable in helping me to clarify my ideas. (*Ceilah* 6/92)

Duncan, another teacher leader, perhaps put it best when he stated his "aha" in the middle of a MASL session: "Now I think I'm beginning to get it," he said. "This isn't about my [doing a] project [in my school]. . . . It's about *me!*"

A common aspect of these discoveries was that they seemed to follow the realization that MASL was not going to "teach" them or, as one teacher put it, "fill my tool box with new leadership techniques." Acknowledging the fog and having the courage and support to plunge into it was essential to generating a leadership growth goal meaningful to the leader and relevant to his or her school. MASL staff steadfastly refused to present an ideal leader type or a formula for changing the school. Instead, members had to listen to their realities, gauge what they demanded, and forge the leadership "mix" that fit best:

> I feel like a child first entering the PET [Pupil Evaluation Team] process. I am now in the evaluation stage . . . that will lead to an increased focus on those parts of my position that "fit" my leadership profile, and "letting go" of other parts that my colleagues are more skillful at and better able to do.
>
> I see myself re-creating my position next year to better reflect my skills and those of my staff. . . . I am still unsure what this will look like and how it will work. This is a new focus of my Leadership Development Plan and I have had few opportunities for feedback yet. . . . (*Margaret 6/92*)

Tamara, an experienced elementary principal, wrote most eloquently about the developmental shifts of the early months of the Academy. She began the Academy as a successful principal; a February 1992 survey of her staff indicated that she was "great. . . . Tamara takes care of everything. . . . You are supportive and caring. . . . You are terrific." But MASL helped Tamara to unfreeze her conception of herself as an ideal leader and come to grips with personal and interpersonal realities that, in her expanded view, were not productive for her school. Here is Tamara's recounting of this period, from her final portfolio in May 1993:

> MASL forced me to examine our performance, and especially my role in making the school work as it did. I began to see some things I didn't like. My feelings became crystal clear when I returned to school having been away for just one day. As I entered my office at 7:30 a.m., I had five teachers lined up at my door before I could take my coat off. Each teacher had a fix-it issue. I felt like the deli clerk at Shaw's Supermarket. . . . "Please take a number. . . . What can I get you?" By the time the last one had left I was exhausted.
>
> They in turn felt great. They had left the problem with me and felt certain I would solve it for them, just as I had done so many times before. I think it was at that very moment that my feelings about leadership changed. Instead of feeling challenged,

I was now feeling abused. Yes, they felt I was great but would I survive this kind of greatness????

[The Academy helped me through the spring to see how I was not helping staff by being Ms. Fix-It. Our Myers-Briggs workshop helped me to understand why I led this way.] My type said: "You base your work on *task accomplishment*." This fit me to a tee: I needed to get everything done myself, Tamara the D for DONE principal.

[What I discovered was that] the D for DONE model, my invisible boundary, was getting in the way of my learning and my effectiveness. I needed to break down this barrier.

The Leadership Academy called into question my own leadership style. Reflection brought about self-doubt and frustration. The strongholds of my leadership, the acts of fixing, of finding solutions, began to feel like weaknesses. I now had to examine what part of my "changeless core" [as a leader] required change and what parts were [helping me succeed as a leader]. (*Tamara* 5/93)

## Summary:
## Starting Points for Growth

We have tried to convey in this chapter the commonalities among Academy members' experiences as they sought a starting point for their professional growth. Their schools offered more than enough student outcome goals around which to form their own leadership development. These, in turn, pointed them toward programs that needed restructuring, propping up, or elimination. But the longer these leaders pondered how they would intercede in the lives of children, the clearer it became that they would need to intercede as well in the lives of adults. Unwilling or unable simply to step in and mandate a new practice or attitude—or even to persuade others of its necessity—members found themselves "befogged" by the complexity and the maze of interpersonal relationships involved in leading improvements in their schools—and in their own leadership growth.

The process of fashioning a plan for professional improvement in this more complex but more realistic world required most to tame their high expectations for themselves as leaders. Coming to grips with the tension between ideal and real was often heralded by an "aha," a discovery that expectations and assumptions for themselves as leaders were overblown or unmanageable. This, in turn, opened the door for members to focus on their own concrete behaviors in leadership situations, both at school and through simulations at MASL sessions. This sequence was instrumental to many members' success at later identifying a manageable goal to change their behaviors as leaders that was linked directly to a manageable goal for changing staff functioning so that student learning would improve.

Finding a starting point for leadership growth proved to be extremely hard work. Ambiguity abounded; it was extraordinarily difficult to "see" one's work, much less one's effects as a leader. In retrospect, it seems that the greatest contribution of the early months of MASL came from members' new capacity to question old assumptions about leadership and to begin building a new, more practical concept of school leadership in which their own behaviors, feelings, and school contexts had a place. Carl, a principal, put it clearly in July 1992 when he wrote,

> MASL has set the stage for me to think and what I'm thinking about is myself, my work, and my own leadership of people there. . . . I was [intended by MASL] to come here to develop myself and to draw out strengths in myself.

We end this chapter with this image of stage-setting in mind, for it characterizes best what the first 5 months of the Academy were about. By unfreezing old concepts and focusing on something real and immediate—behaviors, my school, and me—the leaders prepared the stage for the real process of finding goals for leadership and leadership development.

# SETTING GOALS

## What Specific Leadership Behaviors Will Help My School?

The hard part is selecting a single aspect of what I do as a leader
that, if I can alter it, would really improve how well we work
with kids.

*Hunt 8/92*

**W**e have, it seems, been taught to *think* our way out of problems
and challenges. As Chapter 2 illustrates, much of the early work of
Academy members engaged them in thinking: Analyzing the school's
strengths and weaknesses, reading articles, exchanging new philosophies and techniques of teaching or of student assessment, and
designing programs for students and teachers that would improve
both. But, as we saw toward the end of Chapter 2, the interpersonal
issues associated with *how* leadership makes schools improve introduced a range of facts and factors that were not wholly rational or
subject to the leader's control. These dilemmas were not easily
resolved through thought alone.

This chapter traces Academy members' attempts to set goals for
their own leadership development that were both manageable and
linked to discernible school improvement. In it, we will demonstrate
how most members' LDPs began as relatively neat and orderly
strategies for affecting programs in the schools but soon moved into

the less orderly interpersonal domain as they met the "how to" challenges of making change occur. As these LDPs focused increasingly on how our leaders would *behave* in order for these strategies to have their impact on staff, students, and others, the professional development goals in them concentrated increasingly on less rational interpersonal realities. These, in turn, carried them into the intrapersonal domain, where they struggled with setting goals to understand and control the feelings and thoughts that shaped their interpersonal behaviors.

The important work of writing specific goals for leadership growth took place between the late spring and September of 1992. The Academy staff set some parameters for the process: Goals would be written for changing specific leadership *behaviors* related to school improvement needs identified in the spring; LDPs would incorporate plans for reaching and evaluating the success of these goals; members would implement their LDPs during the 1992-1993 school year. Academy sessions, staff interactions, and a S&D Team for each member were designed to help identify leadership behavior goals and to build these goals into each member's in-action repertoire. The "Leadership Development Plan" framework and MASL's "Curriculum Scheme" were developed to facilitate use of the I-C-I format as members identified goals (see Appendix). The centerpiece of the Academy during this period was a week-long residential institute held at Bowdoin College in mid-July. Its announced purpose was to help members identify and learn ways of "acting in our work settings" that would lead, in demonstrable ways, to the adoption of practices that would improve student learning.

## Starting With Ideas . . .
## Then Moving "Beyond the Cognitive"

MASL requested that all members draft initial leadership development goals in late May and June of 1992 and bring them to the July institute. The spring's assessment activities had alerted most members to the importance of merging goals for working more effectively with colleagues (interpersonal) with goals for improving programs for students (cognitive/programmatic). Thus initial drafts of LDP goals often addressed these two elements. For example,

Abbie, a high school English department chair, identified interpersonal goals of "coordinating communication" and "collaboration" in the service of the programmatic goals of "more efficient use of time," "greater coverage," and teachers being resources to one another:

> I plan to coordinate communication among grade levels in the teaching of language arts; the more efficient use of instructional time will allow greater coverage of material and lessening repetition . . . this will allow teachers to see what's going on in other classes and other schools, allowing them to draw ideas from the best teachers in the system. . . . I think that collaboration and communication are the missing elements in curriculum planning; their absence results in repetition in some areas and gaps in others. That lowers the learning level and keeps understanding superficial. (*Abbie* 6/92)

These first cuts at goals were understandably broad and unspecific. They were conceived in a swirl of Academy ideas and ideals and, as one can see in Abbie's statement, often had a rather academically logical coherence. They were cognitive models that guided members' initial goal-setting by identifying a group or groups of people, some activities they should be involved in, and some outcomes for students that members expected to emerge from those activities. Early drafts of LDPs reflected the full gamut of school improvement goals: science achievement scores, literacy skills at a given grade level, assessment practices for student learning, at-risk student services, integrated electronic teaching and learning technologies, and restructured departmentalized programs and master schedules. In the interpersonal dimension, most LDPs identified goals for team building, collaboration, communication, and shared decision making among their colleagues.

Most of these drafts were excellent first-round efforts. Most members, when pressed by staff to come up with a plan, literally "made a plan" that reflected their current sense of their leadership. When they arrived at Bowdoin and began the work of further specifying these plans, it became clear that they were not only general but that they were also depersonalized. The leaders themselves were not present in most of the goal statements; they were goals for how everyone at school was, for example, going to collaborate but they did not specify the leadership part the leader/writer was going to play to make this happen. The plans were more like *school improvement* plans than they were *leadership improvement* plans.

At Bowdoin and over the summer of 1992, Academy staff and activities, colleagues, and the expectation for a "workable LDP" to be put into action in September shook the substance and foundation of these early plans. As members struggled with converting these cognitively conceived models for school improvement into useful plans for leadership, they encountered the messy realities of limited time, diverted energies, and especially the people—students and staff—who were the central actors in the drama they were trying to influence. If these plans were to help leaders actually change their leadership behaviors, they needed to address how members' interactions with colleagues should change.

This was not an easy shift. Some members shied away from thinking about or even recognizing the interpersonal complexities of their work. Most had little idea initially of how to think about their leadership interpersonally, much less write goals for it. The first step in making progress was to recognize the part that these messier interpersonal aspects of the school played in a leader's success. Here is how Orin, an elementary teacher leader, reflected on this discovery that leadership of change does not "follow logically and directly from the expression of an organizing idea" such as the ones in his initial plan:

> [The Academy so far has led to a] growing cognitive understanding of my beliefs and limitations in knowledge. Rather than thinking in terms of what changes I should try to bring about at the system level, I have begun to think in terms of how my feelings and reactions to how others act toward me might lessen my effectiveness.
>
> The most noticeable effect of the Academy on what I do on the job has been an emerging respect for the complexity of leadership and the school environment. . . . Whereas before I might have assumed that change would follow logically and directly from the expression of an organizing idea, my current assumption is that the road to effective change is winding and full of potholes. I have also come to realize that school change

can be seen as a series of one-to-one and one-to-group interactions. . . . (*Orin* 6/92)

Orin describes the disequilibrium that many members felt at the Bowdoin institute as they struggled to integrate their ambitious but overly idealized first plans with their growing understanding of the interpersonal complexities of their workplaces. As they talked about their own relationships and interactions with colleagues and pondered how their behaviors toward them translated into effective (or ineffective) leadership, their ways became more winding and the potholes more frequent. What helped people like Orin entertain these new complexities—complexities that made the going more difficult rather than less? We have identified three factors that helped most members to "move beyond the cognitive."

First, members' tendency to be realistic, to doubt the validity of overly idealized plans and concepts, contributed to their ability to recognize where interpersonal and logistical roadblocks might appear. By and large, the MASL cadre consisted of educators who were experienced in schools and improvement efforts. They came to the Academy seeking ways to make "real change." They were disposed to move past "unreal" conceptions of what needed to happen and look for down-to-earth, practical, even measurable methods. Craig, a teaching principal, verbalized this aspiration in a June 1992 journal entry:

> The Academy . . . has forced me to examine carefully my role in a complex structure; to begin to quantify my behaviors in such a way that I can use the data I collect to impact the school; to articulate the improvements that I would like to see in myself, in the school, and in the staff in such a way that others can understand them and that they can be measured. . . . (*Craig* 6/92)

A second factor supporting leaders' efforts to move "beyond the cognitive" was the widespread recognition of the huge role "people issues" played in the success of school improvement. Although this point is amply documented in literature (e.g., see Barth, 1991; Fullan, 1994; Lieberman, 1988; Sergiovanni, 1992), most educators intuitively, if not explicitly, know it as well. The Academy fully acknowledged it by constructing the LDP framework around its I-C-I model of leadership. Many, such as this teacher leader, found that this overt recognition of these factors in her success gave her permission to see and accept the interpersonal realities as she set goals. Looking back on her first year in MASL, Tanya wrote,

> The most important lesson I've learned is that the way something is presented is more important than the "something" itself. Does that make sense? It goes along with learning to slow down and accept people as they are, not where I think they should be. Leadership is a people process. (*Tanya* 12/92)

Finally, MASL's sessions, collegial support, and emphasis on reflection encouraged members to see the important interpersonal factors in their schools' effectiveness and in their own leadership actions. Especially at the Bowdoin institute, reflection, writing, and didactic sessions devoted to interpersonal process allowed leaders to understand better the noncognitive forces operating in their workplaces and within themselves. Many needed this retreat setting to recognize and understand the interpersonal dimensions of their schools and their work. As Craig put it in August 1992,

> Only by distancing myself from the day-to-day crises and putting the job, the school, and my roles into perspective, am I able to see how what I wanted to do [as teaching principal] fit in with what was possible to do and what was in line with student progress. . . . I've come to see that perhaps an overwhelmed principal begets an overwhelmed staff and that just maybe a leader who demonstrably "smells the roses" begets teachers who take time to do so, as well, and students who become real learners. (*Craig* 8/92)

This process of coming to terms with the physical and interpersonal realities of school and staff set most members to investigate the interpersonal dimensions of their leadership. Goals that started out as changes in programs now required much greater specificity as a new type of goal: How I need to change my work with colleagues.

## Finding New Definition in the Interpersonal

The many MASL leaders who were able to move beyond a largely cognitive conception of their work found in the interpersonal domain some reasons why logic and persuasion were inadequate to move their faculties into collective action. The Academy staff encouraged this shift over the summer as members wrote successive drafts of their LDPs. At the Bowdoin retreat, we structured activities to introduce a vocabulary for and provide legitimacy to interpersonal reflection. Role-playing, simulations, "rehearsals" of "next steps" with interpersonal situations brought from work were, although sometimes unpopular, nearly universally applauded in this regard (Johnson et al., 1993). Most important, these always included observers, specific feedback, "process time," and journal writing—built-in reflection both at the individual level but often with the S&D Teams' assistance.

These activities helped most members set goals that identified *specific interpersonal behaviors* that would help them succeed in their efforts to affect students' programs. These activities brought members' behaviors to the surface and allowed them to explore their cognitive, emotional, and behavioral impacts on "followers":

> I learn best by role-playing, surprisingly! The times we have done this as part of the Academy has, as a player, given me my gut level reaction and, as an observer, made me think about how I might react if in a similar situation. It has never failed to remind me of "the time that happened to me" or how I reacted to "the time it happened to me." (*Alan* 6/1)

It helped some members to specify the particular interpersonal settings in which they felt they could influence their colleagues most: one-to-one, one-to-small-group, or one-to-large-group. They could then identify skills, feelings, and relationships that shaped their effectiveness with specific people or groups.

When members did this, they frequently discovered discrepancies between what they wanted to accomplish and what they were actually doing. These discrepancies between the "ought" and the "is" proved rich soil for nurturing valuable professional development goals (much as Argyris and Schön claimed in their seminal

1974 work on this matter). Here, a MASL leader examines her interpersonal behavior in meetings and wonders whether the behavioral message she is sending matches her goal for the group:

> Does my behavior support my beliefs? If I believe that people are an organization's strengths, why am I prone to be selectively inattentive [to people in meetings]? If I seek to be respected, why am I not always respectful?
>
> My new goals are to explore:
> - Why am I so judgmental and critical?
> - Why am I most comfortable playing the role of "chief of staff"—as opposed to chief of chiefs? Am I intentionally avoiding risk? Do I fear failure? (*Nina* 12/92)

Nina's questions exhibit a thought sequence that proved very valuable to members as they sought practical goals for their Leadership Development Plans:

> 1. Does my behavior with others support my beliefs and goals for us as a school (i.e., my cognitive plans to improve student learning)?
> 2. What can I change, refine, or reinforce in my behaviors with others that will strengthen my relationship to them as a leader and among them as a team?
> 3. How can I change my own behaviors to make my work with others reinforce my ambitions for them and the school?

This line of questioning became a steady refrain among Academy members, staff, and S&D Teams. It helped fashion developmental goals that brought the cognitive (what I want to accomplish in the school) into better alignment with the interpersonal (how I need to relate to my colleagues to move us toward that) and with the intrapersonal (what I need to do "about me" so that these both can occur).

Once members opened themselves up to this sort of examination-of-myself-in-action, they often found it liberating and even empowering. Acknowledging interpersonal factors put squarely in front of them the significant "people" issues that shape teachers', principals', and parents' success at improving schools. This was liberating, in one respect, because members no longer needed to see themselves, in the old but tenacious leadership paradigm, as solely or even primarily responsible for school improvement. Leaders, in this "more interpersonal" view, did not succeed by thinking up a solution, planning everything out, announcing the plan, and direct-ing, persuading, or imploring other adults to carry it out. A hard look at the interpersonal realities at school acknowledged the wild card role of other peoples' ideas, feelings, personalities, and wills. Here is how one teacher leader put it:

> I've always been good at "answers." I have a hard time figuring out the "questions." . . . I hate to "do" before I *know* what I'm doing. I also like to be "right." The combination is deadly [for a leader] because, to quote a speaker I heard recently. . . . "If we do what we've always done, then we'll get what we've always gotten."
>
> I need to try new things. To quote someone else I heard recently. . . . "Sometimes 'ready, fire, aim' is better than 'ready, aim, fire' because you end up hitting your target sooner!" The Academy gets me doing (firing) faster. It also helps me evaluate what I'm doing, so I can correct my aim readily and get to my target more quickly. "Ready, fire, aim" is the practice that . . . works. (*Duncan* 6/1)

This teacher, like many in MASL, felt liberated to act before he alone had figured out what others should be doing. He simply needed the courage to *ask* his colleagues to help decide what they should do and why. He came to appreciate the value of "trial and error" learning, of being more open with his colleagues at work, and involv-ing them in finding the problem, the solution, and taking action. This work, of course, required Duncan (and others) to develop participative interpersonal skills rather than simply sharpen his cognitive knowledge to come up with the "right" answer to tell staff.

Members also felt liberated by the new focus on interpersonal factors because it permitted them to address persistent "people" ob-stacles in their school improvement work. Many eventually formed LDP goals around supervisory, team, or faculty issues—"people problems" that nagged at them or caused discomfort or anger in colleagues at work. Frequently, these issues made members feel incompetent and frustrated as leaders. By naming them and making them goals for leadership development, some felt they were finally lifting a huge burden from their backs. For example, a high school assistant principal found a major LDP goal by listening to her own feelings about two obstreperous teachers:

> Prior to the Academy, I would feel attacked by them and frustrated by being unable to make them happy. I was constantly frustrated by their treatment of me and personalized their criticisms of anything with the school.
>
> Now I've decided to try to understand where they are coming from instead of making them understand where I am coming from. This has made all the difference in the world. In order to do that I have had to rely on new listening techniques that I was acquiring. I also had to react less, demonstrate empathy, and avoid the need to defend my actions. As a result, I have an entirely new relationship with these two people in particular and other teachers as well. (*Connie* 12/92)

Ironically, the sense of progress members felt stemmed from the seriousness of the challenges themselves. These were *real* stumbling blocks to their leadership, not remote, idealized goals and plans. One high school department head who was working to create a common assessment process for reading and writing throughout her school wrote,

> As I focus on the improvement of interpersonal leadership behaviors, I want to work on skills of collaboration—helping maintain diversity at the same time integrating goals—and consultation with colleagues to reinforce the new practices.
>
> But I know that a major issue for me will be the accountability dilemma: [how to] maintain high morale yet confront the hard questions of why people do what they do and how they could do it better. . . .
>
> According to the Conflict Management Inventory, I am an avoider/accommodater; therefore, I avoid conflict by accommodating others or doing things by myself. . . . This will be one of my challenges. . . . (*Tess* 7/92)

Especially as the summer institute wore on and members came to know and trust each other more, they formed interpersonal development goals around "weaknesses" by working with others. Institute activities in authentic communication skills, conflict resolution, and group leadership and the growth of the S&D Teams all helped in this process. Cicely, a teacher leader, turned a critical eye on how she interacted with others she hoped to influence. She concluded that she needed "now to wrestle with old habits"; these became her interpersonal LDP goals.

> Mine has been a tentative approach to leadership. . . . [In my school] those who raised questions about the structures received flat stares and pat answers. Such critiques were regarded as a waste of time. The question-raisers complicated and prolonged meetings and received the quiet admonition: Don't make more work for us.
>
> I was afraid to ask questions, aware of the general disapproval of upsetting or enlarging the apple cart. . . . I also worried that my questions might offend the administration. When I *was* moved to take such initiatives, I was quick to back down, to accept the pat answer, and to apologize bodily and verbally. Raising questions without pursuing the answers, [I now see], is not leadership. . . .
>
> I find myself now wrestling with old habits. [How can I] ask questions so they won't be taken as assaults . . . [or] carry pointed fingers, whine, and blame . . . [or] condescension [?] (*Cicely* 12/92)

Forming goals around significant interpersonal challenges was very hard work for everyone. It required support, honest feedback, and caring from others as well as a willingness to be honest with oneself. The interpersonal goals most members eventually identified "felt right" to them because they promised to help them work past real challenges with people in their work. A partial list of these include many familiar themes:

- Handling my tendency to avoid conflict
- Dealing with criticism of my ideas in meetings
- Knowing when to stop talking and listen
- Delegating and sharing responsibility

- Checking with others to make sure I'm understood
- Being assertive with my superior as an advocate for my staff
- Making sense when I speak in front of a crowd
- Being a good reflective listener for parents/staff
- Conducting productive group problem solving

## Making Plans Practical:
## How I Need to Behave With Others

The Academy expected all members to implement their LDPs in the fall of 1992 by attempting to "use some new behaviors on the job" that would enhance their leadership effectiveness. Goals that remained as global and conceptual as those listed above were clearly not ready to be operationalized in the behavior of these leaders. At Bowdoin and in subsequent sessions during the summer, MASL staff gave members feedback aimed at helping them specify precisely what they were going to *do* differently when they returned to school.

Some members were able to do this relatively directly, but others struggled long and hard. It proved helpful to examine actual incidents from their past or to consider feedback from colleagues at work if they were fortunate enough to have received some. For example, Karen collected feedback from her grade-level team on her first year as team leader and found that "the one common criticism of my style [from my team] came in a September questionnaire that said I talk too much. I am working hard at changing that . . . and feel [my success] is a natural outcome of being more collaborative and less persuasive." (*Karen* 10/92)

But the greatest leaps in specifying more precise behavioral goals came after they returned to their jobs in the late summer of 1992. Ed, an elementary teaching principal, describes how "the real world" brought him and his LDP up short:

> In many ways, my LDP was the result of the summer session; that is, it was constructed in wonderful vacuum. In spite of my best intentions, a real effort to get ideas from other people, and a sort of agonizing introspection, my LDP came up wide of the mark of what was necessary for me and my school. My goals [to become less directive and more facilitative as a leader through establishing a middle-level faculty team], which made sense at

the time [of Bowdoin], seemed to go right out the window when I got back to school and discussed them with the staff. . . .

These didn't play out because of my basic misunderstanding of the dynamics of team building, my failure to comprehend the interpersonal dynamics that go on between team members and my initial optimism. . . . I also continued to underestimate the amount of time it would take to implement and carry through ideas such as the weekly feedback sheets. . . . [I needed to] take more time to develop the interpersonal team building and provide much more time for planning and preparation of the program itself. (*Ed* 12/92)

Members' initial efforts to act differently generated immediate feedback. Progress came through such repeated "trial and error" efforts punctuated by reflection and redrawing goals in increasingly concrete terms. Typically, interpersonal goals narrowed to one or two or a broad goal such as "listening better" became focused on three or four key people in a single leadership context. This narrowing is illustrated in the words of a teaching principal who had started with the goal of being more "inclusive" and "collaborative" with "school-resistant parents":

Asking questions to clarify and restating are two techniques I find myself more conscious of using. I find a distinct difference now between listening for information and listening for meaning. I am much more conscious of utilizing skills that will better help me understand where these [school-resistant] parents are coming from. . . . (*Doreen* 12/92)

As plans became more focused around specific behaviors, members found it easier to try these behaviors in practice. This in turn boosted their sense of progress. It made their LDP work concrete, their efforts to lead more immediate and practical. The newly specified interpersonal goals gave members a starting place for leading anew in the form of behaviors to use and people with whom to use them. Deborah, an elementary teacher, spoke for many in December 1992 when she reflected on her breakthrough:

[When I started the Academy] I perceived all the hurdles as outside of myself—my principal's attitudes and control, time, the resignation of other people. . . . This year I know I am a leader, and that I need to create leadership from myself. I have taken on projects in the school that I could have done 2 years ago, but because of the perception mentioned above, I didn't.

The turning point for me was meeting with the principal in August and walking her through my LDP. And it wasn't so much that this conversation changed her, but in my taking the risk to share some of the intrapersonal parts and some of my fears, I know now that I can go to her again, that she doesn't perceive my efforts as a threat to anything, etc. It was mainly in the real communication that came out of sharing my LDP that I discovered that we're both in the same boat, and now we both know that we both know!

Knowing that leadership comes from my own efforts, conversations, behaviors, and attitudes, while confronting at times, has actually freed me to begin working for change in the school, instead of waiting for someone to create the perfect leadership role for me. I know I have a certain amount of power to change our school, through projects and other traditional roles, but also through being positive, communicating authentically, and sharing my learning with others. (*Deborah* 12/92)

## Goals for Leading Require Goals for Myself

MASL members found that exploring the important elements of their work with other people engaged them ineluctably in examining themselves as individuals. As this intrapersonal examination progressed, many identified growth goals literally for their "selves." Often they felt more control over these than they did goals for others, for students, or for the entire school. As one principal put it during the summer institute,

What [our S&D Team at Bowdoin] figured out is that I really need to look at myself [to start with]. I found it was really important to look at me and my personal habits and what I have control over. . . . I look in the mirror and I see so many things I like but there are things I see that are driving some people crazy. When I started looking at myself I finally found one thing I had

control of that I know influenced others and how I worked.
(*Margaret* 7/92)

Just as each leader's cognitive/programmatic goals for school improvement needed parallel interpersonal goals to guide his or her
leadership interactions, so did these interpersonal goals need a parallel
set of intrapersonal goals to guide the leader's new behaviors.

The interlocking nature of the I-C-I leadership domains is illustrated in the following teacher leader's LDP. One of Deborah's
programmatic goals was "to educate parents about research-based
program components in our kindergarten program" with the inten-
tion of having parents become more supportive and involved in
their children's learning. As she pondered how, from her position as
a young teacher, she would succeed at this, she worried about
garnering adequate support and cooperation from her more senior
colleagues. This led to an interpersonal goal "to strengthen the
relationship of the kindergarten team by initiating discussion aimed
at discovering program components we have in common that are
based on research." As Deborah reflected on this considerable challenge, she became more aware of factors within herself that were
affecting her ability to succeed. The intrapersonal goal she sketched
out for herself that would, she hoped, enable her to succeed at
"strengthening relationships" among her teammates was "to become more self-assured and have more personal clarity around my
standards for practices I feel are appropriate and supported by
research; to be less dominated by wanting to please everyone."
(*Deborah* 7/92)

Deborah's LDP evolved from program goals to interpersonal
goals to intrapersonal goals; she moved from focusing on impacts
on students to behaviors and relationships with others to how she
as a person affected those behaviors and relationships. In pursuing
the improvement of their leadership behaviors, many members
moved past the behaviors themselves to what it was that made them
behave as they did. Deborah's leadership growth, she believed, was
rooted in developing "self-assurance" in dealing with her colleagues, in achieving "personal clarity" about kindergarten program elements, and in her getting better control over her desire to
"please everyone" so that it would not determine her behaviors so
much. For most members, successfully addressing intrapersonal
goals like these made it more possible to put into action interper-

sonal and programmatic plans and thus reach their goals in these other domains.

Intrapersonal exploration was difficult for many members because it was so new as a professional development activity. Most had not thought about leadership in such personal terms, having viewed it in largely cognitive terms as something one acquires from outside oneself. Academy intrapersonal explorations started with a different premise: that everyone can play some leadership role through cultivating capabilities within oneself. MASL sought to support this self-cultivation through a variety of activities. We provided self-assessment instruments and structured reflective journal writing following leadership events and simulations. Members shared books and articles on leadership, change, and personal efficacy as they discovered helpful ones (such as Barth's *Improving Schools From Within*, 1991; Covey's *The Seven Habits of Highly Effective People*, 1990; Sergiovanni's *Moral Leadership*, 1992; and Wasley's *Teachers Who Lead*, 1991). Most valuable, however, was the chance to talk with other leaders about their own challenges and to reflect on how these had personal relevance. Academy colleagues—and especially the S&D Teams—and the two circuit-riding facilitators became invaluable resources in this respect (see Chapters 5 and 6).

These resources provided concepts and vocabularies for intrapersonal traits that helped members describe aspects of themselves they felt were important to their success interpersonally and cognitively. These became the material of their intrapersonal goals. Discovering a concept and finding that it matched with an aspect of themselves was often seen as a major breakthrough in learning. Margaret, for example, found great relief in the discovery that, despite her "outgoing" appearance and work style as a principal, she was at heart an "introvert":

> In spite of my "outgoing" nature, I am an introvert. I need time to process internally, to rehearse responses, to converse in private before participating in public conversations. At our staff meetings I am not the person to spontaneously share a large number of ideas unless I have had the opportunity for prior reflection. In conflict situations, a major focus of my LDP, I often feel that my initial responses are inadequate or too often are avoidance strategies.
>
> I also feel that I respond most effectively after the encounter when I have had the chance to process the conflict and my

responses to it. I am more aware of why my responses are so different, and so much easier, the next day, on the ride home, or when I wake in the middle of the night. It is the introvert in me processing the information and responding to it in a way that is more natural for me. (*Margaret* 12/92)

Margaret illustrates nicely how members' new insights into themselves led back into the behavioral realm. Once she became "more aware of why my responses are so different," Margaret began to develop strategies for behaving in conflict situations that allowed her to buy the time she needed to reflect and process. Freed from the belief that, as a good principal, she needed to resolve conflicts on the spot, Margaret's outlook on her daily work—rife as it was with the conflicts, complaints, and concerns of all constituents—took on a whole new and more manageable tone. In 1994, Margaret wrote,

[I now see that] conflict is an integral part of our professional lives and an essential component for individual growth. It can provide potential for [a school] to move in a new direction. I am also more aware that I can and do employ a variety of strategies to deal with conflict more effectively. . . . Expanding my repertoire of conflict management skills, to include more than my preferred strategy of avoid-accommodate, has been a goal for me over the past 2 years. (*Margaret* 3/94)

Academy members' intrapersonal LDP goals were as varied as the group itself, yet many fell into one of two general categories. Many members worked on *controlling their reactions* in certain leadership situations. These included quelling feelings of incompetence when challenged, curbing anger or dismissive feelings when confronted with distasteful staff or parent behavior, and fighting the tendency to "side only with the good guys" in discussions. The other major category of intrapersonal goals involved *anticipating problems* and *planning alternative strategies*. These included goals such as Margaret's conflict management practices or learning a specific active listening or authentic feedback technique and identifying situations in which they needed to be used. Many members developed goals of both types, recognizing the need to curb old habits and to develop new ones.

MASL leaders' development of intrapersonal goals required introspection, review of their own actions, thoughts, and feelings in situations in which they doubted their leadership effectiveness. MASL staff worked hard both to encourage introspection and to maintain its linkage to interpersonal behaviors in the service of programmatic ends. A key to succeeding at this was to help members determine, as several put it, "what I have control over and what I don't." Here is a secondary principal's summary of the role of introspection for him and how it needed to be balanced by feedback on behaviors:

> My involvement in MASL so far has helped me focus on what I can change about myself and what I can't or shouldn't. I have been led back over and over to the ideas of defining a goal, setting strategies, doing it and assessing if I met the goal or not. . . . Introspection has led to constructive changes in my behavior or attitudes. . . . I learn best about my own leadership by being observed in action and listening to feedback. I like to tell an observer my goal, have them watch, and then listen to their feedback. A critical friend is my best ally. (*Ira* 6/1)

Once they tuned into their own reactions and habitual behaviors in targeted leadership situations, members began to gain control of their behaviors in those situations. For many, this was a turning point in focusing the LDP around specific, manageable improvement goals. Members, for example, began to identify "trigger" feelings in themselves that signaled the behaviors they sought to change were likely to come into play. One principal described the feeling of "heat creeping up the back of my neck" when some teachers confronted him in faculty meetings. A teacher leader noted that she "shut down" when others around her began disagreeing and another found that he "became more verbal, louder, and more persuasive" when he felt the person he was talking with "resisting or beginning to ignore me."

These powerful discoveries brought a new level of order to members' LDPs. In addition to long and often complex analyses of cognitive or programmatic needs of the school and interpersonal needs of the social settings in which they worked, members now had intrapersonal cues that were directly linked to their behaviors. Their leadership development goals could now be formed around these "in-action" cues to activate new behavioral strategies for working with others. The teacher leader who set a goal of "listening more and persuading less," for example, carried this goal everywhere with him through his daily work, activating it whenever he felt the urge to "persuade other people that my idea is best."

At the bottom of it, there was something deeply empowering about this type of goal. It "went everywhere" with its owner. And it gave members a far greater sense of control over their own growth than either cognitive or interpersonal goals gave them. Orin, an elementary teacher leader who had worked hard to construct an elaborate programmatic goal to restructure his elementary school, expressed this well:

> I was really affected by the focus of the Bowdoin experience (i.e., coming to terms with what we must change about ourselves to "lead" in a community of learners). Lucianne Carmichael [a resource person and ex-principal from New Orleans] is the clearest symbol of this focus. . . . Perhaps she awakened or touched my latent belief in myself. Whatever she did has had a lasting impact, one that is calming, optimistic, confident.
>
> In a way this sense has resulted in my not working as hard on my restructuring efforts (creating the artifacts of my new assessment system for classroom learning), as I realize that the most important work is *within*. I must think, feel, perceive differently if "restructuring" is going to make a real difference.
>
> So, by refocusing on my own changes, I have reawakened my natural confidence and peace. It has also left me feeling less pressure about nailing down every aspect of my work for the year. All in all, a pretty powerful set of happenings! (*Orin 8/92*)

## Summary:
## Generating Leadership
## Development Goals I Can Use

We have traced in this chapter the journey taken by most MASL members from developmental goals that were, at first, broad and impersonal to goals that were concrete and personal. For the many Maine leaders who followed the evolution traced here, this was a journey that progressively gave them a working model for understanding how their personal behaviors affected their schools.

The journey took members from largely cognitive goals for program change to interpersonal goals and finally to intrapersonal goals. Their first conceptions were of goals that defined leadership as changing student outcomes by changing curriculum, schedules, programs, or other school structures. But these left members with too many "how to" questions. These questions led, seemingly inevitably, to exploring how to influence adults in the school (and sometimes outside of the school). Second-generation goals, then, addressed each member's interpersonal skills and strategies. But these led to more questions, this time about how each member could change his or her own behaviors *in order to* improve his or her interpersonal effects. From these explorations came third-generation goals addressing specific intrapersonal challenges that were rooted to the behaviors these leaders sought to change.

As most members moved along the bumpy road of addressing intrapersonal leadership issues, they developed an increasing sense of control over their own effectiveness and development as leaders. Contributing to this feeling were increasing concreteness and practicality to the goals themselves. As our Maine colleagues moved along this road, their goals and LDPs became more and more individualized. Each school context made programmatic and interpersonal goals unique. Likewise, each person's leadership role and personality made the formulation of intrapersonal goals special. Our members, then, spread out all along the route of this journey, moving at different paces and, in some cases, having great difficulty moving "beyond cognitive" or "beyond interpersonal."

In the best cases, leaders were able to identify intrapersonal goals that nested within interpersonal goals that, in turn, nested within cognitive/programmatic goals. In this fashion, the LDP's three layers of goals all worked toward the same end. This nesting proved very difficult in early drafts of the LDP. But as members worked to implement these plans during the 1992-1993 school year, feedback from their professional growth activities helped bring the three domains into better alignment.

# MAKING CHANGE
## Trying New Leadership on the Job

> What an atrocious, sustained effort is required, I find, to learn or do anything thoroughly—especially if it's what you love. A vocation is a source of difficulty, not ease. To do is difficult enough. To be, more difficult still. Both to do and be demand an effort at super humanity. Well, why not? Anything is preferable to the safe side of the line.
>
> Shirley Hazzard, *Transit of Venus* (1980, p. 116)

One year after the Academy began, a teacher leader named Barbara wove this quotation into her journal. Her journey had been typical of many: When she started the Academy, she barely thought of herself as a leader in her high school; but as thinking and planning progressed, she came increasingly to understand how she did—and could—influence her school. Shirley Hazzard's words captured her sense of the complexity of changing how she operated in her school. They articulated especially well the intensity of effort required to "do" and to "be" better than in the past.

Barbara's Leadership Development Plan focused in part on what she called "active listening." Having defined the need for her to become a better listener in facilitating collaboration among teachers, she set out to make herself one. In January 1993, she wrote,

> Silence encourages response. . . . I've bitten my tongue almost
> 'til it bleeds, but I'm learning that to be quiet is often the most
> important part of active listening. In addition, I've practiced
> more appropriate responses to conflict and confrontation. I'm
> learning to see questions as just questions, rather than as per-
> sonal confrontations. In my work I've practiced responding
> with facts, in the belief that most people want my honesty even
> more than they want my reassurance or agreement—and that
> they are best served in the long run by the truth. (*Barbara* 1/93)

Barbara's words illustrate the next stage of the leadership development
journey: making the changes in our own behaviors that we believe will
improve our effectiveness. As she expressed it, this process was almost
always understood as one of trial and error, one in which leaders "practiced" new behaviors and, from this practice, "learned to see" their own
participation and influence in leadership situations differently.

Barbara's selection of Shirley Hazzard's words is telling in several
ways. This step is THE step—the one in which plans and hopes meet
the real world. It requires "an atrocious, sustained effort" and it is
risky. Changing how one behaves with others is not simply a matter
of changing what we "do." It includes also "being" different with
others in relationships that, for many school leaders, have grown
over several years. The school leaders in the Academy found this
"moving into action" phase of their developmental work the most
complex, the most worrisome, and often the most exhilarating.

This chapter traces MASL members' attempts to alter their
day-to-day leadership activities in their work at school. In the first
half, we describe three characteristics of the activities that helped
them enact changes in their leadership behaviors. In the second half,
we report some support activities that proved essential to sustaining
new trial behaviors in practice. As we will see in this chapter, not every
member managed to negotiate the tricky passage from plan to action,
but those who did needed both a way to behave differently and support
activities to give them courage and feedback.

## What Do I *Do* to Be a Better Leader?

The range of activities undertaken by Academy members was
broad, as was the intensity of effort they devoted to making these

activities take hold in their actual leadership behavior. Our evaluations of Leadership Development Plans and portfolios revealed that the activities of members who changed most shared three characteristics: They were context-specific, they focused on interpersonal communication, and they were reinforced by cognitive planning.

First, it helped to specify the work settings, locations, and even times in which new behaviors were to be tried. For many members, it was very difficult to find among all their daily actions a practical way to try out new leadership behaviors because their work days often moved too fast and had too many complex facets. With help from facilitators, S&D Team members, and successively specific iterations of the LDP, many members were able to pin down one or two leadership situations in which they felt they could, by acting in a new way, influence the desired outcomes of their LDPs.

The strategy that helped many do this was what we called an "entry plan," a step-by-step blueprint for behaving differently to help meet their LDP goals over the 3- to 4-week period following an Academy session. The initial entry plans focused on behaviors for the first month of the 1992-1993 school year. Connie, a high school assistant principal, formed her entry plan around her LDP goal to "develop effective listening and questioning techniques (reflecting, summarizing, and paraphrasing)":

[I plan to]
1. Meet with each faculty member individually within the first 2 days before school starts. I will:
  - not rush the meeting. Clearly state the purpose [of hearing each member's plans for the year]
  - ask questions about their plans for the year and listen carefully to the answers
  - not get defensive if negative references are made to last year
  - ask what I can do to help them with their responsibilities
  - clearly explain my expectations
2. Spend time with new teachers, asking questions to learn about them. Clearly explain my expectations to them.
3. Go slowly. Be calm and thoughtful. Review all communication goals and notes prior to meetings. Keep notes in situation journal.

Expected Outcomes: The faculty and staff will begin to see a change in me. [I hope] it will build trust that will be necessary for the change process and team building. . . . (*Connie* 8/92)

Here, Connie clearly links new behaviors she wants to use—"do not rush," "listen carefully," "do not get defensive," "be calm and thoughtful"—with an outcome that is intended to benefit the whole school (and which was tied to student outcomes through her LDP). Although the behaviors themselves remain somewhat generalized, she identifies types of people and interactional situations in which her new behaviors will need to come into play.

Ozzie, an elementary principal, devoted his LDP to developing a teacher evaluation plan. His interpersonal goal emerged from difficulties he had confronting others with negative feedback. His new leadership activities fell into two contexts in which he "tried to model openness and honesty with the faculty":

1. At faculty meetings I have made a point of letting the teachers know when I think they have room for improvement. In the past, I have been quick to praise, but have avoided pointing out problems. [Provides an example of poor recess supervision.] Last year I would have mentioned this somewhat meekly and thrown out a veiled threat to put more teachers on playground duty. This year, I clarified my concern and asked the teachers to come up with their own strategies to assure that the playground is adequately covered.

2. During my weekly meetings with each faculty member I have been commenting on the positive things I have observed in the teacher's classroom as well as pointing out areas that I feel need improvement. I have been doing this in a much more direct way than I have in the past. [Describes an instance in which he suggested a teacher change his schedule but the teacher did not do so.] I found out a couple of weeks later that he had not made any change in his schedule. Instead of letting this slide, I approached him again [using new behaviors] to find out why he didn't make the change. He told me that he just hadn't had time, but that he would start to have math in the morning beginning in January. (*Ozzie* 12/92)

By identifying where, when, and with whom new behaviors would be used, Ozzie, like other MASL leaders, pinned down which new behaviors he would try. The entry plan was a helpful tool for many in this respect.

The second characteristic that aided in the success of these activities was to frame them around interpersonal, and particularly communication, behaviors. If plans revolved around, say, new listening behaviors, as in Connie's case, or new follow-through behaviors, as in Ozzie's case, leaders could implement these in numerous situations on a daily basis. Because interpersonal communications are so central to school leadership, "locating" a specific set of steps to alter one's own behavior in certain communication settings proved extremely beneficial to behavioral change.

Ida, a high school assistant principal, targeted five quite specific behaviors to work on as she took part in restructuring committee meetings. Her LDP goal was to build more staff ownership in restructuring through communicating better and pushing her own personal agenda less overtly. Her entry plan included the following:

> In the restructuring team meetings, [I will]:
> - think before I talk
> - show genuine interest in what others are saying
> - expand upon what others say, but in a way that is not interrupting or finishing others' sentences
> - mentally identify opposition and pause before I react, particularly focusing on not becoming defensive
> - include the less assertive people in the discussion
>
> The outcomes I want are each person feeling connected to the team; inner confidence that I have accomplished my goal of beginning to be a better communicator. (*Ida* 8/92)

In a similar vein, Margaret, an elementary principal, devised a step-by-step conflict resolution strategy to use with a difficult staff member in regular one-to-one meetings. Other principals planned strategies for becoming more collaborative with staff and/or parents by "using more consultative language" with staff and parents, starting "discussions" among others rather than directing communication, giving more positive feedback, and avoiding rushing into situations "and saving the day all the time."

Teacher leaders' plans, although often aimed at becoming more assertive, benefited as well from the specification of new behaviors to be used in common school situations. Eleanor, for example, found it useful to write "an entry plan for every week" in her drive to "every day be more proactive than reactive (as I have been for 40 years)." Another secondary school teacher leader wrote about her leadership of a group of eight teachers working together on a grant to implement a reading-writing assessment plan:

> Even though we are a cohesive group, there are real differ-
> ences—not just in subject matter—of how we teach and even of
> what high expectations and student accountability mean to each
> of us. The crux of the development of myself as a teacher leader
> is to become a consultant teacher using cross-disciplinary skills
> and content as a vehicle for coordination as well as to improve
> key communication skills.
>
> It is here that my interpersonal/intrapersonal goals mesh. I
> want to maintain morale, involvement, and the collaborative
> spirit of the group at the same time that I fight my desire to avoid
> conflict with people when it may be useful to confront some
> differences. I and the other members of the group will have to
> confront each other on questioning techniques and assessment
> of student learning. This implies, too, that I am opening myself
> up to others' scrutiny.
>
> Therefore, I have to trust myself in two ways: to stand up to
> and be able to respond and/or argue with others about my
> teaching and to have the courage of my conviction enough to
> stand up to others and question what they are doing and why.
> Even now, the magnitude of this task is pretty scary to me. . . .
> (*Tess* 7/92)

Other teacher leaders designed plans to clarify their roles and relationships to their principals or superintendents so they and their peers could move ahead in planning their changes in curriculum and teaching. Karen, for example, framed her new one-to-one consulting behaviors with her principal as learning to "be the sand, not the pearl."

Still other teacher leaders worked on facilitative and collaborative behaviors. Frequently, their activities sought to make them less critical of teacher colleagues who did not share their ambitions or work habits. Cicely wrote that, in her efforts to become more accepting and less critical of colleagues' attitudes, she was working "not only on my self-expression [toward them] but also at acknowledging and understanding the messages and the messengers. . . ." Becky's plan to break down old animosities within her faculty focused her activities on

> accepting negative attitudes/behaviors of others, but I am working on finding out what is behind the attitudes and behaviors of adults just as I do with students. Expressing interest and offering to work with a staff member whose attitude/behavior seems negative benefits both of us and helps us communicate and work together. I have found this understanding and collaborating to be helpful to me and believe it makes me a more effective leader. (*Becky* 12/92)

Other teacher leaders' activities aimed at "shifting conversations" with colleagues to the topics they wanted to influence, at coalition-building with colleagues one-on-one in preparation for meetings in which decisions were to be made, and at generating agendas and follow-through lists from team meetings to guide their groups into real action.

A third characteristic of successful leadership change activities was that they were often initially learned at a cognitive level, then gradually worked into existing behavioral repertoires. Conventional learning activities often gave members an intellectual frame for their new behaviors. For example, reading Stephen Covey's *The Seven Habits of Highly Effective People* (1990) was a popular source of ideas for interacting differently with people at work, as was Roland Barth's *Improving Schools From Within* (1991). Similarly, workshops on Total Quality Management, effective teaching, and "the change process" introduced strategies for teaming, long-range planning, and mentoring that helped structure the action steps of LDPs. Members also used each other and conventional research procedures to locate specific resources to share with staff and colleagues to advance their LDPs (such as frameworks for authentic assessment and for alternative high school scheduling). Finally, some found it useful to cull ideas from the school improvement literature, such as the planning-evaluation cycle or lessons from the Coalition for Essential Schools principles and research materials (McQuillan & Muncey, 1993).

These cognitive lessons tended to be easy to learn but difficult to implement in LDP activities. They needed to be translated to the important settings and the particular people MASL leaders were attempting to influence. The professional growth activities themselves tended to involve "going and getting" new information or "consuming" a book, workshop, or course. The carryover of these activities into practice required that the leader mold the cognitive lessons to the demands of his or her own leadership situation, discarding what seemed inappropriate and, most important, applying it to a specific meeting, person, or task. Ceilah, for example, used her Myers-Briggs Type characteristics to understand better how to deal with more "conservative" colleagues:

> [The Myers-Briggs Type Indicator showed me that] I like action, excitement, and change. The scores on my leadership evaluation [from colleagues at school] confirm that people view me as an enthusiastic and energetic leader. . . . [But] I think it is important for me to periodically evaluate my leadership to see what effect it is having on other people who might want me to be more conservative. . . . I will have to balance my desire to act authentically with my desire to be a good listener so that I won't be perceived as an overbearing presence. . . . I don't want my presentation to obscure my competence. (*Ceilah* 5/93)

Tamara, an elementary principal, structured her LDP around the "three acts of courage of an Authentic Leader" presented by consultant David Sanderson:

- Facing the harsh reality
- Owning up to our contributions to the problem
- Being authentic even in the face of disapproval

> These three components of Authentic Leadership exemplified all the behavioral changes I needed to make; the roadblocks, struggles, and shifts of my LDP. I saw in this style of leadership the "new image" I was yearning to understand and become. It was to be the focus of my major learning. Mrs. Fix-It could be no more. (*Tamara* 5/93)

Another principal read extensively about active listening techniques (cognitive preparation), then rehearsed some of these with her S&D Team and in Academy role-plays (interpersonal preparation), and

finally worked them into her meetings with specific people at school
(interpersonal behaviors-in-action).

These three characteristics of leadership development activities—specifying work contexts for them, focusing them on interpersonal behaviors, and working from a cognitive model—helped
Academy members put their LDPs into action. In the final analysis,
how- ever, this process was much more imprecise and unpredictable
than most expected. As Chapter 3 described, goals and LDPs were
frequently in flux as members' understanding of their leadership met
the realities of their schools. LDPs developed in the relative safety of
Academy sessions, office, or home often had a half-life of a week or
two—just long enough for the leader to try to change his or her
behaviors once or twice. Then it was back to the drawing board to fit
the plan more closely to people and situations at school. As important
as the plans and activities were, the support and feedback of colleagues
made it possible for this continual adaptation to take place.


## Keys to Growth:
## Courage, Support, and Feedback

Enacting change in one's own behaviors on the job was risky
work in several respects. It meant acting differently among people
who were, in large part, comfortable with the way members usually
acted. It often meant having other people begin to behave differently
with one another and with students. And the justification for these
changes was often subjective, ambiguous, and open to debate. For
the many MASL leaders who engaged in such change, the inherent
riskiness in it sent them looking within themselves for both the
courage and the confidence to act:

> Learning to lead requires a willingness to fail and to take risks—
> a willingness to embrace change, and a willingness to accept
> new ideas. Learning to lead requires one to know and accept
> oneself and to acknowledge that one's power to change begins
> and ends with the self; that the ability to influence others'
> behavior lies in practicing what one preaches. (*Nina* 8/92)

How did MASL members manage these risks? We came to
appreciate the need for continuous preparation and reflection in

supporting and critiquing our members' new acts of leadership. Our recipe might read: "four parts preparation and reflection to one part action." Partner activities, simultaneous to and eddying around acts of new leadership, needed to be organized to help each leader prepare "how I'm going to behave differently tomorrow" as well as evaluate and reflect on how well those behaviors worked once "tomorrow" had passed. Without these partner activities, we doubt that many of our members would have been able to sustain the effort and courage to make new behaviors take hold. Three particular types of partner activity helped members to enact their LDPs:

- *Getting My Head Straight:* Preparing philosophically and psychologically for taking the risk of changing behaviors in the public arena of school and community
- *Setting Up a Safety Net:* Rallying support and encouragement from others to provide good ideas, practice, and faith in these efforts
- *Using Feedback to Make Sense of My Efforts:* Making arrangements to collect feedback to use in evaluating, reframing, and continuing these leadership change efforts

We address each of these important intrapersonal learning activities in the rest of the chapter.

### Getting My Head Straight

As LDPs rounded into focus and entry plans were formulated over the summer of 1992, Academy members increasingly realized that they were expected to start their new school years *acting differently* among their old colleagues and students. This realization prompted among most members a "commitment check," some serious and sustained intrapersonal reflection on their conceptions of themselves as leaders and on their commitment to changing their practices. Academy staff and now Academy colleagues expected each member to *actually act* on the plans in his or her LDP!

Through the late summer and fall, S&D Team sessions and informal talk among Academy colleagues and the MASL facilitators buzzed with an undercurrent of anxiety. Members seemed to be summoning, in Nina's words, the "willingness to fail and to take risks . . . to know and accept oneself and to acknowledge that one's power to change begins and ends with the self." For many this meant coming to terms with their own power and ability to influence others and the responsibility that entails. Orin, a teacher leader, demonstrated how distinguishing "in my own mind" the boundaries of his power and control helped him understand where he could succeed with his new leadership strategies and where he might not:

> Another classic pattern for me is to dwell on how powerless I feel and as a result begin to withdraw. In this instance [with my co-teacher], though, I tried to separate in my own mind those elements I have control over and those that I do not, hoping in so doing that I would be able to limit my worrying to the former.
>
> Lo and behold, it worked! I have begun to seek out connections with other colleagues who are interested in similar issues and let go of my desire to try to make my colleagues/co-teacher do anything. My stress level is lower and paradoxically my colleague seems more upbeat about things. (*Orin* 12/92)

The act of writing out their planned changes often helped members clarify the rationale and purpose of their actions. These frequently took the tone of a pep talk and the flavor of a professional platform (similar to those described by Osterman & Kottkamp, 1993). Many members appreciated the staff's insistence on writing in journals and repeated drafts of LDPs as these literally made them "get my head together." Belle, a high school principal, reinforced in writing her resolve to begin valuing "the person" as much as "the task" as she began the 1992-1993 school year:

> Most significant in my learning over the summer was the confirmation that shared leadership and shared decisions take enormous amounts of time and checking for understanding and caring about how the people are feeling in the roles and decisions with which we are wrestling. It's not just *what* we are producing, but *how* we are functioning.
>
> For years I felt I had to and wanted to produce without monitoring the personal cost to me, although it was *sort* of a factor I considered for others. For lots of personal reasons, I

pushed myself onto levels of success and attainment [and it cost me personally].

I know that *how we feel* as participants, as fighters, as supporters, as followers, as leaders, as resisters, as challengers is vital to keep the momentum going (my usual concern) but also to ensure that the person thrives and is valued and is satisfied and is given a chance to grow and has the time to laugh and to assess the progress. (*Belle* 8/24)

MASL records are filled with countless "sermons to myself" of this sort aimed at clarifying plans, positions, and purposes. They played an important part in establishing these leaders' self-confidence and clarity of purpose before—and often during—their attempts to behave differently. Writing also helped them think through complex and emotional situations and draw together their convictions about what to do next. Here, Ursula describes how she handled the emotional aftermath of an administrative team meeting:

At first I was angry. I then sat down and wrote out the true issues. I see them to be power and control and that I want everyone to agree with me (probably hoping that they think I'm a good guy) and that the final issue was what is right for the children of [this community]. I discarded the issue of me as irrelevant once I saw it on paper. It's nice to be liked by everyone but not critical to the children in [this community]. Once I decided I could let go of my anger and focus on how to make the situation right, I made a plan [for my leadership that worked]. (*Ursula* 12/92)

Much of this "getting my head straight" activity found its way into the intrapersonal section of members' LDPs. The value of intrapersonal reflection, in fact, became more and more apparent as they discovered the benefits that emerged from examining their own talents, foibles, beliefs, and feelings. MASL leaders who most successfully grew in their work tended to be those whose grasp of themselves was both accurate and comfortable. The following extensive excerpt from Abbie's August 1992 LDP illustrates how members' frank assessments of themselves intrapersonally led to a conviction to function better interpersonally.

## *Intrapersonal Dimension*

*Goals:*

1. To start the change process by changing myself, especially to recognize that change will come when I can remain open to all ideas.

2. To stay healthy, rested, and strong throughout the year.

3. To have faith in the good will and good intentions of my colleagues.

*Assessment:*

At my best, I can stay composed, open, and generous, but when I'm overtired or ill I lose that composure and become judgmental and defensive. That posture just further offends those colleagues who were suspicious of my ideas in the first place. And I can hardly blame them; as long as I see change as something that I do to them, there is little hope of our finding common ground.

*Plan to Grow:*

The intrapersonal plan has to be concentrated in two areas: the physical and the psychological.

In order to stay rested and healthy I must follow a regimen that includes regular sleep, good nutrition, and fitness. I have made a good start in that with membership in a fitness center; I have conscientiously included more fruits and vegetables in my diet and have cut down on fats; I have tried to get at least 8 hours of sleep a night. This is all fairly easy in the lazy atmosphere of summer, but the real test will come in the fall. . . .

The psychological dimensions . . . will be harder to monitor because it will mean that I must look at my colleagues in a new way: I must truly believe that they mean well and are not being obstructive out of stubbornness or laziness. In order for me to truly believe this of them, I must concentrate on those parts of their work that I truly admire. . . . I intend to keep a journal in which I reflect on those strengths and document the ways in which each of them could help me to become a better teacher. I plan to use this writing to change my way of thinking: "Don't wait to think yourself into a new way of acting, act your way into a new way of thinking."

*Evaluation:*

I'll have two objective gauges of evaluation. First, I will monitor my health and fitness weekly and second, I will keep a journal of my reactions to my colleagues that will give evidence to any real change in attitude. (*Abbie* 8/92)

The intrapersonal dimension of the LDP became, for Abbie and many others, the core of their plans to change because it gave them a place to "get their heads straight" with themselves. Toward the end of the Academy, Harris, an elementary school principal, put it succinctly when he wrote, "I continually go back to what Lucianne Carmichael said [at the Bowdoin institute] about looking at yourself and that you need to change your behavior to become a better leader—you cannot change another person's behavior without looking at yourself." (*Harris* 12/92)

## Setting Up a Safety Net

A second partner activity that supported behavioral change was having regular contact with trusted colleagues that focused solely on leadership growth experiences and issues. Most members found these safe but challenging collegial contacts among their S&D Team members and the Academy facilitators. Some developed them, as well, with colleagues at work.

S&D Teams provided many the constant, dependable, and trusted network of fellow travelers that is often missing among school leaders. Their power to help was rooted in the simple fact that their purpose *was* to help each member grow. Over the first 8 months, we devoted time and activities at Academy sessions to creating open, supportive relationships and a vocabulary for leadership growth among team members. The formal evaluation of the Academy found that S&D Teams, for many, became continuous and readily available sources of advice and sounding boards for emotional outlet. Because Chapter 5 explores the experiences of S&D Teams, we include one example here simply to illustrate their effect. Margaret, a teaching principal, found her S&D Team helped her keep the following realistic perspective on her abilities to change others:

I don't need another project to put in place to be a more effective leader: What I do need is a continuing look inward, an honest

evaluation of *my* skills, attitudes, and beliefs. . . . My S&D Team
and my Academy colleagues have allowed and encouraged me
to be open and, at times, vulnerable. [As I come to see myself
more accurately,] I am coming to rely on the feedback and
support from them. (*Margaret* 8/92)

S&D Teams and Academy sessions provided a protected interpersonal setting in which members could explore and rehearse new
behaviors to use in their work. Early in the Academy, the entire group
had agreed on some ground rules that would support such exploration. These were formalized as guidelines for our community
of learners and revolved around supporting one another, challenging one another to grow, and respecting confidentialities.
These understandings made it possible for members to engage in
behavioral experimentation designed to extend their leadership
repertoires.

This often occurred in simulations and role-plays. Most helpful
were those in which members brought scenarios from their own
workplaces to act out, which gave them a chance to practice the new
behaviors they hoped to incorporate permanently into their leadership. One teacher leader expressed the value of this form of active
rehearsal and assessment in the following manner:

I learn best from hearing, reading, and talking about new ideas
and strategies. Then I need time to practice these ideas/strate-
gies in a safe setting. I then mentally visualize the application
in a real setting. After the "real thing," I need to be required to
honestly assess my success and appreciate direct feedback from
fellow participants and observers. (*Cicely* 6/92)

From these role-plays and rehearsals, members came to value various types of preparation for difficult situations that would reduce
the uncertainties and risks. Cicely, in her portfolio, wrote, "To bolster my courage and resolve, I practiced scripting my thoughts and
presentations [for this difficult meeting]. . . . [I also] quietly enlisted
the support of several influential friends [before the meeting hap-
pened]." (*Cicely* 5/93)

For some members, the two full-time, on-call facilitators were a
powerful safety net in the risky work of leadership change. This was
especially true for members whose S&D Teams did not coalesce to

provide the support needed. Because the facilitator role is taken up in Chapter 6, we will include only one example of their supportive function. Here, a teacher leader describes a meeting with Isaac, one of the facilitators, in which his questioning of her approach to her LDP helped her recognize her own style and how to use it to her advantage as a leader:

> The meeting with Isaac marked a real turning point for me, with implications for my own growth that may well move me more quickly into being a self-actualized leader. . . . We got into an in-depth discussion about my dislike of forms, boxes, structure, detail, etc. [related to developing the LDP].
>
> Through some excellent questions from Isaac, I suddenly came to grips with the fact that rather than having no structure [as I had always thought of myself], I had an internal and highly developed style of learning/teaching that I really just needed to specify and translate [for others I was leading in this more traditional setting]. This was incredible and exciting for me, and one of those moments that I will look back on as a landmark in my growth. (*Victoria* 5/93)

Yet another activity that proved a safe way of thinking through new behaviors and strategies was sharing journal entries. This happened regularly with facilitators and staff. Response journaling with S&D Team members or with other colleagues was a helpful way to work through questions and dilemmas prior to action. One teacher leader shared this entry from her journal with an in-district colleague:

> This journal will be good for me—when I put things down on paper rather than just keep thinking about them I tend to want to deal with them better. Somehow once it's written down, the issue or problem becomes real. [The issues I need to work on are the following:]
> - avoid avoidance
> - delegate
> - strive for self-awareness
> - remember situational leadership
> - reflect on what it means to be an NT [one of the 16 Myers-Briggs types] (*Faith* 12/92)

A high school principal used writing as a means to structure his interactions at work more thoughtfully. Writing gave him distance and time to reflect on the action which, in turn, permitted him to "share" more equally in the group's deliberations:

> Not thinking enough about the results of what I say has gotten me into more hot water than all the defensive, nonlistening, and all other behaviors [I've used] put together. Clearly this needs to be a major point of emphasis and has not been. . . .
>
> I take notes at all meetings, date them, review and file them. I try wherever possible to write shorthand notes before I speak at meetings. It may only be two or three words. This is prompting me to ask why I am saying something at a meeting. Often someone else will say what I was about to say. In our shared decision-making model, ideas are much more effective when they come from other people [not just from me, the principal]. This is especially true because the ideas come out more fully formed than the way I would have presented them. (*Ira* 12/92)

Finally, a few MASL leaders successfully extended their safety net to colleagues at work. This proved a very potent approach to their professional growth because it combined the development of support mechanisms with visible risk-taking in the workplace. This simultaneous activity modeled "learning while leading." These leaders, through sharing their own LDP goals and seeking advice and support from colleagues at school, were setting new levels of openness, trust, and permission to risk among those colleagues themselves (and children as well). Irene, a middle school principal, described her experience this way:

> One of the first steps I took in implementing my LDP was writing a letter to the junior high school faculty explaining my LDP. This included outlining my cognitive, interpersonal, and intrapersonal goals.
>
> The cognitive goals portion of the letter was easy and fun to write [regarding moving the school toward being a "Quality School"]. The interpersonal goals and intrapersonal goals were much more difficult to address. It's never easy to admit, publicly and to people with whom you work daily, that you have areas that you want to and need to improve.

However, the feedback that I received from the letter was extremely positive. Many of the comments were oral and could be summarized by the following statement: "Thanks for the letter. I'll let you know what I think from time to time." Others did not directly refer to the letter, but instead gave me feedback about various meetings and activities in the following manner:

"Nice job of running the faculty meeting, it felt honest and open. . . . I look forward to more opportunities to build a relationship of trust—as a parent and as a staff member. It's not always easy to admit you're having a problem with something. Your openness allowed me that opportunity to be open back. None of us is perfect and everyone can use some help now and then. Thanks for the help. . . ." (*Irene* 1/93)

Although Irene's big step was, as a principal, to share her developmental plans with her faculty, teacher leaders often began by sharing theirs with their teams or departments or, importantly, with their principals. Deborah did this and found that the benefit of being open with the principal about her ambitions

wasn't so much that this conversation changed [the principal], but in my taking the risk to share some of the intrapersonal parts and some of my fears, I know now that I can go to her again, that she doesn't perceive my efforts as a threat to anything, etc. It was mainly in the real communication that came out of sharing my LDP that I discovered that we're both in the same boat, and now we both know that we both know! (*Deborah* 12/92)

For both principals and teacher leaders, sharing their own growth plans with colleagues, although risky, often built relationships that proved essential not only to their own professional growth but also to their schools' improvement.

## Using Feedback to Make Sense of My Efforts

A third partner activity to support behavioral change was collecting feedback and arranging regular reflective times to use it. Feedback on members' leadership behaviors was made possible by the specific entry plans, the trusted colleagues, and the safe settings described earlier. MASL staff explicitly encouraged, facilitated, and, eventually as part of the portfolio-exhibition exercise, required members to collect direct feedback on their behaviors to use in evaluating their impacts. In addition, workshops at Bowdoin and after introduced members to "straight talk" feedback conferencing techniques.

Belle, a high school principal, saw her S&D Team taking an active role observing her at work. She planned to structure feedback instruments and observation methods to focus on the growth of her skills running meetings more effectively:

> To gain these skills I will have to continue my research and self-analysis of meetings and requests of assessment from people who I respect for their own leadership skills and their honesty. I will need to develop a stronger "Atticus Finch" style of viewing issues from another set of eyes.
>
> I will rely on the S&D Team to assess the clarity of the written and spoken directions and questioning techniques. I want to develop an instrument that can quantify the skills that are OK and those that need remodeling. I will rely on them to assess that the discussion, consensus, and action steps allowed ample sharing of ideas and tackling of the conflicts so that when decisions are made that they can be supported rather than be subverted or unnecessarily reopened.
>
> Because the team cannot be in every meeting nor be able to predict the explosive ones, I'll rely on filming, recording, and journal entries to assist us. I can also use the trusted staff members to be critics too. Their comments I'll need to document in the journal as well. (*Belle* 6/92)

In another case, a high school principal was fortunate to have on his staff a member of his S&D Team. They developed a system for assisting him on a regular basis to become a better "editor" of his own words and interactions in leadership situations:

> Myers-Briggs confirmed what I learned from observations of me by critical friends and my own introspection. Not thinking enough about the results of what I say . . . has gotten me into more hot water than all the defensive, nonlistening, and all other behaviors put together. Clearly, this needs to be a major point of emphasis [in my LDP]. . . .

I continue to debrief with Eleanor after meetings. She frequently scripts them. We meet at least once a week now on a semiformal basis to review each other's progress. I am logging the first 5 seconds of most defensive conversations either by type of encounter or by logging the phrase that got me [on the defensive].

I am trying to take time to decompress after being yelled at. I stop, take the phone off the hook, clean, shoot baskets, talk to someone about nonschool topics or otherwise go away for a while. . . . (*Ira* 12/92)

The other major source of feedback for members was their colleagues at work. The Academy pressed members to collect some direct evidence of their effects on both colleagues (regarding their interpersonal goals) and student outcomes (regarding their cognitive/programmatic goals). Although difficult, most leaders succeeded in retrieving some data about their initiatives and behaviors. The most helpful of these were regular feedback mechanisms that asked about specific behaviors such as this one developed and used by Kim, an elementary team leader:

Dear Friends,

I am trying to improve my listening skills. Would you complete this listening tool so I become a better listener for you? When we have had conversations . . . (please circle yes or no)

1. Do I maintain eye contact (but not stare)?  Y  N
2. Do I show you I am listening by my body  Y  N
   position, gestures, and short responses
   (uh-huh)?
3. Am I silent long enough to let you get your  Y  N
   point across?
4. Do you feel I hear the ideas, intentions, and  Y  N
   feelings as well as the facts?
5. Do I accept statements I may not want to hear?  Y  N

Do I ask questions that
6. help you with your thoughts, feelings,  Y  N
   experiences, and opinions?
7. draw you out as a colleague?  Y  N
8. clarify what you have said?  Y  N

9. Am I too judgmental in my responses?          Y     N
10. Do I paraphrase what you have said without     Y     N
    judging (agreeing or disagreeing)?

Thank you *very* much!

Kim

Direct feedback, either from MASL observers or from school colleagues, was extraordinarily valuable to Academy members who collected it regularly. Their success at benefiting from this third partner activity, however, often hinged on the other two partner activities. They often needed to "get their head straight" to summon the conviction to risk collecting feedback in the first place. Most needed the safety net of Academy sessions and trusted colleagues to reflect productively on what that feedback meant and how their subsequent leadership actions might need to change.

## Summary:
## Taking New Leadership Action

The Maine school leaders in the Academy sought to develop their own leadership effectiveness by practicing new behaviors. Although we have much to learn about this critical step in the leadership growth process, members found that three things helped them put new behaviors into action: specifying work settings, locations, and times that new behaviors would be used; concentrating on specific interpersonal behaviors with particular people; and clarifying the behaviors and their intended effects through studying cognitive models.

We found, however, that factors beyond the new activities themselves often spelled the difference between use and nonuse, success and failure. Three types of partner activities—"getting my head straight," "setting up my safety net," and "using feedback to make sense of my efforts"—often made it possible for these Maine leaders to summon the courage and the clarity of mind to begin behaving differently. In the next two chapters, we describe further how the S&D Teams and the facilitators helped members make this crucial transition from plan to action.

# WITH HELP
# FROM COLLEAGUES
## The Colleague-Critic Team

> At the risk of sounding like I'm at a tent revival, my life has
> changed dramatically because of my work with my S&D Team.
> I felt totally supported and listened to, but without ever being
> given the opportunity to get away with anything.
>
> *Charlotte* 12/93

S&D Teams were the lifeblood of the Academy experience for most
people; they were "a stroke of genius," as one member put it. Rooted
in the belief that school leaders need a safe but challenging environment to help foster professional growth, the teams were designed to
offer such an opportunity while leaders were implementing their
Leadership Development Plans in their schools. For many, the S&D
Team component of the Academy became a major vehicle through
which members reflected on their actions, sought advice, brainstormed ideas, rehearsed future scenarios, and gained the emotional
support needed during intense times.

MASL staff saw the primary purpose of this small group as
assisting each member to grow as a leader. This would require the
members of each team to know the personal and professional needs
and the local circumstances of each person's workplace. It would
also require support and encouragement mixed with honest, direct

feedback and assistance. Group process skills such as these would be learned, relearned, and practiced during Academy sessions and S&D Team meetings. It was the staff's hope that ultimately some members of the Academy would be able to transfer these skills and create such a supportive environment in their schools.

This chapter describes the structure, development, and functions of the S&D Teams and how the staff, and Academy members themselves, nurtured the maturation of these teams over the course of their time together. We provide examples of how the teams functioned, examine the value of such professional development teams in schools, and, finally, identify some of the factors that contributed to the effectiveness of the S&D Teams.

## The Origin and
## Life of the S&D Teams

The formation of these colleague-critic teams was a delicate matter. The MASL staff, in the spring of 1992, found themselves steering the formation process despite their conviction that collective mentorships are best developed in a mutual, voluntary matter. Over several Academy sessions, staff put forward criteria for S&D Teams: They would be diversified by roles, grade levels, gender, and years of experience, yet members would need to be geographically close to one another; and they should if possible avoid previous friendships that might inhibit new learning. Members were encouraged to discuss team formation and to suggest teammates to the staff. The staff then juggled those requests to create teams of three or four people. These decisions were based on one fundamental criterion: Good S&D teammates would both *support and challenge* each person's professional growth as a school leader. Then the hard work of team formation began.

The Bowdoin summer institute became the first major opportunity for teams to work together in a concerted fashion. During this time, a strand of the Academy curriculum focused on small group and team development issues as well as interpersonal, communication, and conflict management skills. Academy staff saw these group process activities as critical to both the success of the S&D Teams and to members' understanding of group issues when they later implemented their LDPs in their schools. At the institute, members lived and worked with one another, with many giving uninterrupted focus to the outcomes of the week and building trusting relationships with one another.

At Bowdoin, the two facilitators worked with the teams for the first time introducing their roles and beginning to develop a working relationship with each group. The facilitators monitored each team's initial struggles as it began to coalesce as a group and establish norms of behavior. It was a critical tone-setting time, as individuals began to imagine and put into practice how they would work together as a team during the upcoming school year.

These discussions continued throughout the week and resulted by Friday in a formalized "S&D Team Agreement" that described each team's operational ground rules and established a schedule for fall meetings and visits to each other's schools. One team, for instance, agreed to the following:

1. Abide by the ground rules established by the network:
   - We will participate at our own comfort level.
   - We trust that what we say is confidential.
   - We trust that our motivations are based on good intentions.
   - We believe that attending our meetings is important.
   - We share responsibility to "make it work."

2. We will meet by mutual agreement, generally at Vista Junior High, from 4:00 p.m. to 7:00 p.m.

3. Anyone can call off a meeting due to stormy weather; we will establish storm contingency dates in our calendar.

4. Each meeting will include sharing time at the beginning of each meeting, some social element, an update/focus on each person's LDP, time to set an agenda for the next meeting, and an evaluation of what was accomplished at the meeting.

5. We will honor each member of the group by listening carefully and not interrupting.

6. We will rotate the leadership for each meeting.

Such well-formulated ground rules helped teams get off to a good start once the hectic pace of school picked up in September. As one of the members of this team stated in his journal:

Our S&D moved into the fall, carrying out an early and aggressive meeting schedule. Before the end of September, we had visited each other's schools, observed our teammates in action, and established an understanding of each other's LDPs. (*Bill* 10/92)

Throughout the school year, most S&D Teams functioned as small groups of colleague-critics supporting the work of the individuals in the team. While individuals concentrated on implementing their LDPs in their schools, S&D Teams met between Academy sessions to focus on the successes and setbacks of their professional growth plans. Team members met at all times of the day and evening in a variety of school and nonschool settings. Some met every 2 weeks; others every 5. Peppered between these team meetings were phone calls to one another, journal writing and sharing, chats over a meal, open letters to team members, a newfound comaraderie at professional meetings and conferences and visits to one another's schools.

Woven throughout this tapestry, the two facilitators traveled the countryside attending S&D meetings whenever possible. During these meetings, the facilitators were often seen as "a ghostly presence"—a person who was there to participate but not to control or set the agenda for the team meeting. Occasionally the facilitators were full participants in discussions, but often they took a back seat and observed interactions, took notes, documented progress, and provided feedback to the team on their work together. At other times, the facilitators acted as the "conscience" for the team, reminding them of their established ground rules or Academy expectations.

It was during these months while members "worked their plans in their schools" that colleagues began to learn to work with one another by being there to listen, to reflect, to ask questions, to share vulnerabilities, and to lend support and encouragement. The challenges of the school year shaped the number of times teams met, the focus of their time together, and the way team meetings were conducted. Teams that had crafted strong and specific "agreements" tended to stick with them, especially if they hit the ground running with meetings and visits to each other's schools scheduled the first weeks of the school year. Others, especially those that had chosen not to meet early on, had a more difficult time establishing S&D meetings and school visits as their calendars began to fill or their teams struggled with formation issues. For most teams, finding the time to observe each other in their workplace was a constant challenge mitigated by the ever-pressing demands of the school day and questionable building-level or district support for such professional development activity. Such factors shaped the content, process, and ultimate value of the S&D Team structure for its members.

## How the Teams Worked Together

In the S&D Teams, many members' cognitive and theoretical understanding of their goals began to move into the murky waters of the interpersonal realities of the school. The teams tended to struggle with this transition in five major ways. These focal points shifted from person to person and dilemma to dilemma throughout the school year as trust developed and the team found its own way to help its members.

First, members used S&D Teams as sounding boards for specific issues they faced, either in the formation of their plans or, more frequently, once the school year had started and they were struggling with implementing their LDPs. Tess, a teacher leader, encountered a difficult challenge in an important meeting at work. Her S&D Team played a vital role in the formation of her next steps:

> I spent a considerable amount of time with my S&D Team members and another MASL member trying to figure out how to handle the situation. Everyone agreed that I needed to confront the person so that she would recognize that her behavior and her comments were not productive. . . .
>
> This kind of confrontation is very difficult for me. I tend to want to ignore any conflicts, to hope that the other person will just snap out of it, and to be very nervous about future meetings with the group and/or with the person with whom I have had a confrontation or the potential for one.
>
> My S&D convinced me that I needed to do something, though. I could have tried [to have the grant committee] deal with [the conflict], but since it is part of my LDP and I am the facilitator for the grant, I knew that it was incumbent on me to do something. (*Tess* 12/92)

Assistance in confronting issues in their work usually came not through the prescriptive process of giving answers or talking about how it should be handled but through consultation and problem-solving strategies. These people moved forward in their own thinking and feelings so that they were able to find possible solutions within themselves and their own resources. Often teams brainstormed possibilities, role-played, or rehearsed a conversation as a way to address the tricky, behavioral issues of leadership. Especially on teams that met frequently and became more intimate, members were able both to ask colleagues to "hold me to my promises" and to give one another direct feedback and opinions.

A second way in which S&D Teams functioned was as a "laboratory" to actually work through how to confront an issue they were facing. Doreen, a teaching principal, faced just such a challenge late in the fall:

A crisis—obviously unanticipated—took me to my S&D Team desperately needing to role-play a meeting with a very supportive parent about an issue with her child that was very critical. The parent had always been positive, and this meeting was going to be threatening to her. The team [and our facilitator] helped me to attempt to figure out possible variables and strategies to the anticipated meeting. [After acting out different scenarios,] the next day, I felt better prepared. The support of the group around this one was critical for me. . . .

Skills that I had been working on that made that possible, in my estimation, included improving listening skills by practicing with Margaret and Ivan [my S&D Team members]. The practice wasn't just in the sense of how many times we role-played, but also in the attention paid during conversations to my role and what I wanted to get out of any discussion. (*Doreen* 1/93)

It was during such meetings as these that the skills and techniques (e.g., "straight talk," authentic feedback, and others) learned, practiced, and reinforced during role-plays and simulations at Academy sessions bore their fruit and helped members develop alternatives to the specific challenges they faced.

Such opportunities for rehearsals also took place around less controversial but no less anxiety-producing situations. Shelly provides one such example scheduled to take place during an upcoming S&D meeting:

> Fran and I plan to act out a real-life situation when we next meet. She needs to practice interviewing for an assistant principal, and I want to practice interviewing for that role. We will try to video the mock interview, and Alex and Laura will be our resident critics. I am also putting together a resumé for my team's reaction, including letters of reference. (*Shelly* 12/92)

The third function of S&D Teams was for members to push one another to confront tough questions arising from the workplace, from self-assessment data, and from efforts to lead in new ways. As Bill, a teacher leader, put it:

> I recognize that my ability to use Academy resources, at this point, centers on using my S&D Team as evaluators of my progress. I also appreciate the type of probing questions I'm asked as we discuss LDP work. My leadership practice is improving in light of that evaluation. (*Bill* 8/92)

A fourth way S&D Teams worked together was by providing their members a safe haven in which to converse freely about issues important to them but too uncomfortable to talk over in their schools. Team meetings became a vehicle to talk about educational issues they had been exploring and wrestling with introducing in their schools and as a place to talk about the stressful interpersonal relationships they often faced. The following discussion points out the importance of such opportunities:

Cicely: The S&D Team was a unique opportunity for frank and open discussions about people and issues in a protected setting. I'll miss that in my life. It takes a structure for me—an upcoming meeting with a time to reflect and prepare for it.

Ira: Me, too. I've felt a freedom to talk about issues that I'd never feel at work. I feel freer to take chances here.

Ed: Many people at work often wouldn't care about these issues. As an administrator I have to do a lot and can't talk about the tough things with staff. I need a place to [vent] safely! (6/93)

Finally, S&D Teams met at members' schools and observed team members in leadership activities in their schools. The purpose of such visits was to give each leader feedback on how their new leadership behaviors were or were not affecting those they worked with daily. Observations and feedback in pairs, as a team, or with their facilitator became concrete, specific, and personal. Members came to know the realities of another's leadership challenges. This school-based focus vastly increased the value of subsequent conversations because they were centered in specific behaviors, particular people, and workplace issues. One teacher leader talked about the insight he gained from such observation of his work:

> For my growth as a leader I counted on the input that my S&D could provide. In preparation for that input, I prepared a full list of behaviors and skills that I wanted them to comment upon as I directed the conference. . . . [A team member's observations at the conference] provided genuine support as I sought to succeed at a goal I had worked toward for many months. Likewise, my work as a department head and an agent for change in our district curriculum coordination was covered by the other members of my team and by [my facilitator]. These opportunities to discuss in detail and with first-hand knowledge my leadership efforts provided me with invaluable opportunities to reflect and grow. (*Bill* 5/93)

## The Value of S&D Teams

In their conversations, reflective writing, and evaluative statements about the Maine Academy for School Leaders, members consistently pointed out the integral role that the S&D Teams played in their personal and professional growth. The preceding examples provide glimpses of the qualities that members appreciated in their work together as teams:

- A structure that supports mutual growth
- A common experience and language as the basis for discussion
- Meaningful connections with colleagues across school roles and grade levels
- Emotional support and encouragement
- Challenging questions and conversations

- Honest and straightforward feedback
- A sense of trust and confidentiality that promotes reflection and action

In many cases, these qualities grew not from team members' unqualified support of each other but from a mixture of support and tough, challenging questions:

> My S&D meetings were initially meaningless to me as I was completely unfocused and drifting. At Bowdoin I began a very poor rough draft of a personal and portable LDP that I could take anywhere. . . . The school year started and I was still not focused in my LDP work or actually very honest with Tanya and Harris [team members]. I was putting them off until I was ready to really look at my leadership. I used excuses. . . .
>
> Then I had a fire lit under my pants by my very brave colleagues Tanya and Harris. They were operating on a different level and needed my commitment to be on a par with theirs. I had not been honest with myself or them. I had been doing so many things wrong that would sabotage my effectiveness as a leader. . . . This confrontation was what I needed to get going and get involved in something beyond me. . . .
>
> [Looking back,] the biggest help to me was the S&D Team—just going and hashing over issues I'd been through. This was after we came to our understanding as an S&D. For me the whole atmosphere changed then. It was like slapping me around a bit. The team helped me help myself. [They helped me to see that] the nonverbals I use really affect people . . . how I turn people off. Tanya and Harris were brave enough to bring these things to my attention. That made the Academy work for me . . . I felt more invested in it. (*Jason* 5/93)

Members like Jason found in their S&D Teams a rare opportunity to look honestly at themselves—blemishes and all. The synergistic mix of support and challenge often enabled a level of authenticity to emerge that kept professional growth on the front burner in the face of the daily bombardment of shifting school priorities.

For some teams, maintaining such a mix was a challenge. In such cases, the "laboratory" aspects of the Academy experience helped individuals and teams to function more effectively. At Academy sessions, teams were encouraged to examine their own behaviors, group process, and communication issues. This process is demonstrated in the "Assessing Our S&D's Activities and Process" questionnaire, which enabled teammates to share perceptions about one another's participation and its effects on the group (see the Appendix). One member later reflected on this activity as a turning point in the work of her team:

> The S&D format worked well, especially after the session where we rated the qualities of our team first as individuals and then as a group. For us, this opened up a different and much more honest approach to each other. (*Faith 6/93*)

Such conversation was invaluable as a means of checking self-perceptions against the perceptions of others. Based on these discussions, adjustments were often made in the team that raised their awareness, enhanced their functioning, and moved people toward more authentic relationships with one another. The lessons from the S&D experience were valuable, as well, in "real" situations in the workplace:

> [My S&D Team has] contributed to my increased understanding of how I have handled conflict in the past and why the resolution of those events has not been very satisfying. The conversations we have had every 2 weeks have added greatly to the experience for me by providing a frequent setting to receive support, discuss difficulties, and connect with the broader educational community. The assistance I got from the S&D Team made a major difference in how I handled the situation with [a teacher at my school]. (*Orin 5/93*)

As the 1992-1993 school year passed, members and staff became increasingly adept at offering genuine feedback to one another. This proved important as the Academy shifted into its final phase and another valuable outgrowth of working in professional teams was revealed. During the spring of 1993, members worked on their summative Portfolios of Leadership Learning. Artifacts and evidence of their learning had been collected right along. The question then became how to make sense of it all. Team members worked with one another and their facilitators putting together portfolios and exhibitions that would later be shared. Trudy, a facilitator, wrote about one such session with an Academy member in her journal:

> We began with a huge unorganized pile of materials and were able to put it together into an understandable format. Ida, without realizing it, clearly articulated her major learning. She identified herself as "an Academy success story" and talked about how she had learned that she couldn't solve all problems by herself. She described situations where she has allowed staff members to take charge of the decision-making process with good results. I, playing the devil's advocate, asked, "What if you hadn't had good results?" She was able to talk about different strategies she would have used. As she talked, I outlined what she was saying and informed her when she was finished that she had just outlined her narrative section of the portfolio. I sensed the meeting was dramatically helpful to Ida. She is the kind of person who needs to think through a process before she can jump into it. Our discussion allowed her to do that. (*Trudy* 4/93)

Working through this assessment phase with others helped to formalize the learning that had taken place and affirm its value publicly.

## What Helped S&D Teams to Work

Achieving a level of functioning that made S&D Teams valuable in these five ways was not easy. Academy members had to work at creating effective teams that met their needs. In fact, some teams only reached a level of consistently effective functioning as the Academy was ending. Variations among them stemmed from the personalities of team members and the fact that teams needed time, commitment, and trust to form on their own.

Some members wanted MASL staff to take a stronger hand than they did in making their teams function:

*Eleanor:* It took us hours and hours to figure out how we were going to run our meetings. We could have used a lesson in how to do this. . . .

*Ed:* Yes, it would have been helpful to define S&D Teams more clearly and tell us so we could get going sooner.

*Cicely:* I balk at that! We just finished saying it took some of us a while to get past the *expected* S&D goals and norms to *ours.* I'd encourage everyone from the start to work at their own S&D Team needs. (6/93)

The two facilitators, through their observations of S&D Team meetings and follow-up processing, were able to help members struggle with such differences to better understand and develop useful team practices. Strategies such as regularly scheduled meetings; steps to foster collaboration, trust, and communication skills; and mechanisms for feedback were common topics of conversation. As teams matured, they became increasingly able to monitor their own working norms and procedures and to adjust practices to suit all three or four members.

Over the life of the Academy, several factors helped member groups evolve into effectively functioning S&D Teams:

1. *Stated purpose*—the clarity the team members expressed in their discussions about their short- and long-term goals and needs for themselves as individuals and for the team as a whole;

2. *Willingness to explore the I-C-I model*—the degree to which people moved beyond the most comfortable level of interaction, the cognitive, and were willing to share their intrapersonal strengths and weaknesses as played out in their interpersonal relationships with others in their schools;

3. *Trust to become colleague-critics*—the ability of individuals to set aside traditional roles and fears to work as colleagues dedicated to both challenge and support the beliefs and actions of others so that they can grow as school leaders;

4. *Ground rules that encouraged authentic conversation*—the structure that guided meetings, their frequency, and their content helped to determine the depth to which people were able to work with one another;

5. *Ongoing connections*—the number and variety of contacts between meetings helped team members to keep each other abreast of the latest developments and better enable them to hit the ground running when they met as a group.

For most teams, development ebbed and flowed over the course of the 16 months together based on the nature of particular issues, individual and group commitment, the pressures of the school calendar and workload, the constant struggle to achieve balance between one's professional and personal life, and the willingness to take risks. The pattern was captured in this comment:

> Our first meetings were carefully focused and involved the working out of our own goals. The goals were diverse; they were developed for our own educational agendas in our own respective schools. We did not really move from this task orientation until we began sharing stories about personal conflicts, both past and anticipated. . . . The important interactions developed around this situation and quickly transferred themselves to our professional reflection-and-problem-solving sessions. (Hoffman, MacKenzie, McCabe, & McDonough, 1994, p. 40)

## Summary:
## A Culture for Professional Growth

The S&D Team was conceived as a personalized, close-to-the-action support mechanism for leaders' growth. Members' team experiences showed that clearly stated and agreed-on goals and expectations often created a structure that met their own learning needs. Teams were productive when members committed to regular meetings and to visits to one another's schools to observe the work environment and each other in action. When members kept in touch with one another between sessions by phone and mail and showed up for those meetings with dilemmas and issues from their leadership experience, teams rallied around them, offering a mix of support and tough questioning that helped them devise their own "next steps." Such highly functioning teams became growth experiences in and of themselves. They supplemented personal development through engagement with the team and its own growth as a supportive entity.

S&D Teams evolved into the primary learning vehicle of the Academy for many members. The trust and comaraderie that developed in these small groups formed a culture for professional growth.

Here, in their own feelings and style and at their own pace, individuals could share thoughts, anticipate future actions, and rehearse the behaviors necessary to implement their ideas. Although the nature of each team varied significantly, nearly every Academy member noted how positively their team had affected him or her. We came increasingly to admire and respect the power of these collegial groups to help ambitious leaders move forward. Shelly said it best:

> The most powerful aspect of my learning in MASL is to be in the company of so many colleagues with such great ideas. Every time we meet I come away with new insights and energy about my work and my profession. In practice, I know that several heads are always better than one, and when colleagues are allowed the opportunity to problem solve and create in a collaborative environment the outcomes are much more rich and varied. (*Shelly* 6/92)

# FACILITATING
# LEADERSHIP DEVELOPMENT

[The facilitator was] an annoyance in the beginning . . . another someone to answer to. . . . Now my facilitator is an ally, a colleague, friend, resource, impartial bystander, one that offers another perspective.

Johnson et al. (1993, p. 44)

Hiring two people to work exclusively with members of the Academy on their professional development was one of the innovations built into MASL from the beginning. The rationale was simple: School leaders needed ready access to thoughtful, knowledgeable people *when and where* they were striving to change their leadership behaviors. The facilitators were to foster reflection among Academy members about specific practices they sought to improve. However, as the opening quote indicates, the benefits of the facilitators' efforts often took time and hard work to develop.

In this chapter, we focus on the creation and nature of the position, the evolution of the role and the relationship that developed with Academy members, and the value they saw in having a person whose sole responsibility was to assist them in their leadership development. The chapter concludes with some of the issues faced by the facilitators as they worked to support the leadership development of Academy members.

## Two Facilitators in an Evolving Role

The Maine Leadership Consortium, the sponsoring organization for the Academy, hired two facilitators in December 1991. The
two individuals, Trudy, an elementary school principal, and Isaac,
a secondary principal, became part of the staff developing the
program for the Academy. After June 1992, when they began full-
time work, Trudy and Isaac became the primary staff contacts for
the two regional networks of school leaders. Trudy summarized her
initial impressions of the position this way:

> Within 10 minutes, I'd made a decision. I'd apply. I obtained the
> guarded support of my superintendent and my family and de-
> cided to go for it. After all, people told me I was a good adminis-
> trator. I had vision, I could sell my ideas, I could build ownership,
> and I was a master at compromise and keeping people happy.
> Most days my staff loved me. I had a gnawing feeling they were
> getting a bit dependent but maybe it was just battle fatigue! I
> could readily teach someone else survival skills. I'd spend my
> time giving other people answers or connecting them with peo-
> ple who had the answers. I'd brush up on my reading and come
> out a year later more up to date on theory. . . . Surprise! Surprise!
> It didn't turn out that way. (*Trudy* 5/93)

The Director and Assistant Director, both of whom were part-
time staff, worked collaboratively with the facilitators to define not
only Academy activities but also their roles. Here, Isaac reflects on
the evolving nature of his work:

> What was most important was not the content but the affective
> areas, especially our modeling of behaviors and the experiential
> aspects of the work. That is the component that makes us signifi-
> cantly different and an evolutionary step forward in comparison
> to other institutes and conferences. Of course it is also at the heart
> of building a community of learners and leaders. The challenge
> to us as facilitators will become the maintenance and fostering
> of that comaraderie over time and geographical space. I hadn't
> really thought of it in quite this way but the S&D teams will
> function as the cells of the body of the community with us as the
> connectors and determine in many ways the picture and essence

(our DNA) of the whole Academy that emerges over time. (*Isaac* 7/92)

The tasks associated with the role of the facilitator evolved with the Academy members' needs. During the Academy's first phase, "Assessing My Leadership," the staff worked to structure and organize the Academy into two regional networks and 16 S&D Teams. The facilitators' first contacts with members were organizational; they led activities designed to introduce the fundamental principles of the Academy's framework and to build working relationships with and among members. Because both facilitators continued in their principalships through June 1992, they devoted their scant energies to clarifying expectations and assisting members individually with the assessments of their schools and the formation of initial developmental goals.

During the second phase of the Academy, facilitators became more intensely involved with the S&D Teams and individual members as they created first drafts of their LDPs. It was during this time that teams began to work together establishing their ground rules and testing out the nature of the colleague-critic relationship with one another. The facilitators worked closely with individuals on their plans, helping them assess their own needs and establish personalized goals and action strategies.

With the beginning of the school year came the critically important third phase, "Changing My Behaviors." Built on the premise that changing one's leadership behaviors within the school context was the most difficult but ultimately the most rewarding aspect of professional growth, the facilitators began to "ride circuit" from school to school and meeting to meeting, working with individuals in a coaching relationship. They spent numerous hours on the phone maintaining contact between site visits. Observing and working with members while they were in the midst of their schools' daily action formed the heart of each facilitator's function. Through these conversations, problem-solving sessions, and rehearsals for upcoming situations, members were able to test their espoused values and beliefs against the hard reality of their actions.

As members became embroiled in altering old habits, the facilitators offered to serve as observers and mirrors to help members reflect on their own actions. Trudy and Isaac sought not to provide answers, but to help open the way to greater self-understanding—

intrapersonal knowledge, action, and growth. An important piece of this reflective learning was its documentation. Feedback from individuals, journaling, structured narratives, and team discussions all became vehicles through which facilitators and individuals worked together to continually monitor, assess, and oftentimes refocus their growth as leaders.

The final phase of the Academy, in the spring of 1993, offered a more formal opportunity for facilitators to work with members to assess their learning across the three dimensions of the I-C-I model. They met with members during S&D Team meetings and as individuals. The primary focus was on helping members make sense of the journey undertaken over the previous year and a half. Facilitators talked about the process of portfolio development, conferenced about highlights and stumbling blocks along the way, provided feedback on early drafts, and in some cases even modeled how to engage in the process of reflection and documentation.

Over the course of the Academy, most members came to know their facilitator well and looked forward to conversations and visits. In the best cases, such as the session Victoria reports here, these contacts made lasting impacts:

> Last Thursday, December 17th, marked an incredible learning experience for me. . . . I want to credit [my facilitator] with doing an excellent job of listening and probing. It was his questions and attentiveness to what I was saying that enabled me to get a handle on an area of my leadership that will definitely make a difference in my effectiveness.
>
> For several years now I have used myself as my example of an effective leader, and have measured others against my own model. This continued with MASL, and, while I have been learning in a general sense, I have not felt that I was in the midst of real and dynamic growth. I was focusing on some personality change issues, rather than really exploring and reaching beyond what I know. . . .
>
> Enter December 17th. Was it [my facilitator]? Was it a new S&D Team? Was it my diet? Was it being on tape [because an outside evaluator was observing]? Was it the weather? Really, it was me, in the mood and with excellent support that moved me into a space where some light bulbs really went on. . . .

> This meeting marked a real turning point for me, with implications for my own growth that may well move me more quickly toward the self-actualized leader. . . . In summary, we got into an in-depth discussion about my dislike for boxes, structure, and detail. Through some excellent questions, I suddenly came to grips with the fact that rather than having no structure, I had an internal and highly developed style of learning/teaching that I really just needed to specify and translate from outdoor/experiential into a more traditional approach. This was incredible and exciting for me, and one of those moments that I will look back on as a landmark in my growth. (*Victoria* 12/92, 5/93)

Not endowed with superhuman qualities, the facilitators constantly wondered how best to enhance the efforts of so many individuals to reach the goals of their LDPs. Although any one person cannot be all things to all people, facilitators needed to blend a variety of talents and skills in their effort to respond to each member. The Academy's formal evaluation report concluded that

> overall, the facilitators were appreciated, respected, and relied on to a great extent by most participants. A quality facilitator-participant relationship is a result of shared experiences and time which, in turn, results in a high level of trust. Mutual acceptance of and respect for each other as professionals, leaders, and learners is necessary. Facilitators/leadership must model the ability to set goals and engage in self-assessment. They are empathic, flexible, and constructively critical. They are knowledgeable about and able to engage in effective group process. They are familiar with the participant's site and strive to keep participants focused on specific leadership goals. The facilitator provided the one-on-one emotional support and feedback unique from other Academy components. (Johnson et al., 1993, p. 76)

The needs of Academy members varied. Some sought a facilitator to "fill my toolbox" of leadership techniques whereas others wanted "patience and cooperative leadership for allowing me to make some of my own mistakes while providing structure enough so I won't hang myself" (*Alex* 8/92). The Academy evaluation identified five elements of the facilitative role:

- Acting as a resource for information
- Providing assistance in reflective practice and self-assessment
- Helping to focus on specific goals and leadership behaviors
- Providing theoretical knowledge about school leadership and educational change
- Strengthening interpersonal, cognitive, and intrapersonal skills (Johnson et al., 1993, p. 43)

Most of these qualities are captured in Orin's mid-year self-assessment. He both summarized his facilitator's contributions and specified how he expected to benefit in the future:

> First, I will ask [my facilitator] to assist me in developing a list of potential elements in my portfolio and advise me in the ongoing documentation of my work at school and in the Academy in order to lay the groundwork for successful certification and eventual employment as an administrator. [He] has also been helpful in his role as sounding board and counselor regarding my conflicts with my colleague and I anticipate continuing to draw on his judgment and expertise as I work through further difficulties. I propose that when he visits my work site these two subjects be given roughly equal time in our discussions. (*Orin* 12/92)

The strength and ultimate success of such plans for professional growth rested on the relationship that developed between the Academy member and the facilitator.

## The Key Ingredient:
## Building Authentic Relationships

Both the formal MASL evaluation and the staff's assessment concluded that success in facilitating leadership growth rested in *building authentic relationships* with each school leader. As with all human connections, the quality of these relationships varied dramatically from person to person, situation to situation, and over the passage of time. The most productive of these evolved over the course of the Academy to a point in which discussion about a

member's learning was open and trusting. Ira, a high school principal, put it well in an interview with Isaac:

> The most useful thing to me has been the development of my
> muse. I don't know if that is quite the right term, but when I'm
> talking to you I feel like there is a third person in the room and
> that person is analyzing my behavior and yours and why we are
> both here and what is going on and is helping me to figure out
> the best course of action.

When asked what usually helped him focus on what is most important in terms of his leadership development, he responded,

> I don't know if feedback from others is [most important] or my
> own analysis of that feedback. But I know that without that
> feedback from you and other people my analysis is worthless
> and if I just take in the feedback and don't use it to change my
> behaviors it also is useless. (*Ira* 12/93)

It took time to reach this level of openness and trust. Relationships evolved slowly as both the leader and the facilitator explored
how best to use the facilitator to enhance learning. For example,
Ceilah wrote to Isaac, "You were very open about your role and
some of your uncertainties about it. I didn't know how to use you,
what to do with you, what the expectations were for me." (6/93)
    Sincere conversation was essential in building a relationship
that allowed the facilitator to provide support to the Academy
member. This was due, in part, to the responsibility placed on
members to shape their use of the facilitator to meet their own
professional development needs. However, it was also attributable
to the very nature of schools:

> We're not accustomed to this kind of attention and help . . . close
> to my work, me, my school. As my facilitator you were ready to
> be open and honest, but it was my school environment that
> isn't. . . . (*Bill* 6/93)

Four factors seemed to influence the relationships formed by the
two facilitators and members. The first was simply the number and

nature of one-to-one contacts between facilitator and members. These varied widely from a few to many in a year's time. Affecting the frequency of contacts were the distances facilitators had to drive for their site visits and members' readiness to have an "outsider" intrude into their work lives. Types of contact ranged from listening and consulting to observing leadership behaviors, from prodding further growth through conversation and written feedback to acting as a resource person. The differences that existed in members' understanding of the I-C-I model, their own learning styles, abilities, and expectations further complicated the issue of appropriately determining when and how to intervene as a facilitator.

Second, and closely related to the first issue, was the facilitator's maturing understanding of this form of experiential learning. They were learning along with members that facilitation necessitated different ways of relating than are typical in many traditional settings. As Trudy recently stated when reflecting on this issue,

> We were moving from positions where our authority and role were clearly understood by others to one where we were responsible for creating and selling a new concept of learning. Facilitators and members were products of a learning system that rewarded figuring out the one right answer or at least what the teacher would accept as a right answer and giving it back in an appropriate way. We had all succeeded by these rules. Now we were saying to members, "figure out what you need to learn and tell us." They as students weren't sure how to do this. We as facilitators were uncomfortable waiting to be asked for help. They often had difficulty asking. We had difficulty knowing how to help them ask. (Trudy 2/94)

The third factor in building a working relationship was making time and preserving energy to work on leadership development among the pressing day-to-day demands of schools. The facilitators' challenge was to remind members of their commitment to growth without having the facilitator assume responsibility for the members' learning. There were certainly times when the facilitative role became that of an "enforcer," pushing members to keep their own growth and development on the front burner in their lives. Facilitators often worked hard to connect the daily concerns faced by school leaders to the interpersonal and intrapersonal dimensions of the individual's LDP. It was through a refocusing on these process-oriented dimensions that each issue or crisis contained the potential for the individual's further growth as a learner and leader.

The final and perhaps most challenging factor centered on the continual struggle faced by many members of the Academy to link their leadership development to improved learning for students. The facilitators raised this issue time and again. As one principal stated,

> Relating leadership skills to student outcomes called for me to focus on student achievement rather than educational management issues—to look at long-term impact on students related to my leadership as opposed to day-to-day custodial/keep-the-building-standing issues. This has been my number one challenge. (Johnson et al., 1993; Appendix F, p. 18)

For some, and especially for the teacher leaders whose LDPs arose out of classroom-based goals, the connection was readily apparent. For many, though, the linkage was more difficult, and seemed to increase in difficulty as the leader became more removed from daily contact with classrooms. Too often it was easy to gloss over this important linkage and it became exasperating for some to be brought back to this basic requirement by their facilitator. By the close of the Academy, this had contributed to the fraying of some relationships.

As both facilitators and members of the Academy learned, the most helpful relationships were evolutionary in nature, the needs and understanding of each person. The most productive facilitator-member relationships were characterized by the following:

- Having the time to talk and share experiences with one another
- Providing insights and demonstrating emotional support during professional struggles
- Experiencing success from collaborative problem solving
- Experiencing and sharing success with one another when an LDP goal was attained
- Demonstrating sensitivity and flexibility in responding to the changing needs of the Academy member

## Making Sense of the Role of Facilitator

Sixteen months after the Academy began, the two facilitators had logged tens of thousands of miles visiting schools, S&D Team meetings, and homes. They chatted for hours over the phone and spent many more hours responding in writing to journals and LDPs. They focused their efforts on helping to keep the connection alive and vibrant between and among the members of the Academy. In Isaac's final portfolio, he reflected on these countless hours and conversations and came up with this potpourri of role descriptors:

What is a facilitator within the context of such a professional development program?
- A circuit rider who travels from school to school
- A colleague-critic willing to ask probing questions, while being supportive of the person
- A demonstrator of new practices and behaviors
- A mirror through which others reflect on themselves
- An enforcer of Academy expectations
- A conscience to remind others of the value of their own professional development
- An active listener
- A helper and resource provider
- A steward of our efforts and ideals
- A confessor to nonjudgmentally listen to shortcomings, fears, and self-doubts
- A stimulator of conversation and dialogue
- A documentor of growth and development
- A reflector on both the individual's and the Academy's evolving patterns of leadership development (*Isaac* 5/93)

Although Isaac's writing focused on the ways in which he worked to support the growth of school leaders, Trudy, the other facilitator, explored how her thinking about the facilitator's role and her own learning about leadership had dovetailed:

Good leaders are facilitators. They create conditions where people can constantly grow and learn. Through modeling and honest communication, they grant permission to try, to succeed and to fail, to share their successes and failures, to refine their efforts and to try again. As a facilitator, I learned this again and again. I repeatedly went to meet with someone who would share their problem of the moment with me. When I was ineffective, I commiserated or suggested what I would do. When I was helpful, I clarified, asked questions, and allowed (or even forced) people to come up with their own answers. The first approach resulted in a person feeling incapable and uncommitted. The second generated understanding, enthusiasm, and investment. (*Trudy* 5/93)

At its most potent, the facilitator role modeled some effective practices that members could use in their own leadership. Two members capture this ripple effect in a June 1993 conversation:

*Ed:* It was very helpful to have [my facilitator] in my school, clarifying issues with me and just to sit and [talk]. It was great to have someone who was on call! Having [my facilitator] come in and observe me with my faculty taught me I could use others in the school for this type of resource.

*Eleanor:* He was an incredible resource for us too . . . to have someone focus on no one other than me and my leadership and give me feedback! Now, my colleagues are getting into each others' classrooms.

*Ed:* The same for us. With more people coming into our building in this way, we've been looking at ourselves a lot more. (6/93)

Incorporating the principles of facilitation into their work in schools, some members transferred their own learning experiences in the interpersonal and intrapersonal realms to their leadership strategies with colleagues. In this manner, some members came to see the central challenge of school improvement to be facilitating learning among their fellow adults at school.

## Summary:
## Supporting the Growth of School Leaders

The facilitators were seen by Academy members as the glue that helped to hold this confederation of leaders and learners together.

They helped to provide and maintain the connection among members through their travels from school to school, team to team, and person to person.

Where trust grew and increasingly honest conversations prevailed, the facilitator was able to help leaders refine their developmental goals, risk new behaviors, and turn a frank eye on their own efforts. For the facilitators, this work was a constant balancing act between being supportive and raising challenges. In the end, what benefited members most may have been the rare chance, as Margaret put it, "to experience . . . a real value in having someone come to my school that I can talk to who's not linked to the district . . . [someone] who I can talk to honestly was so very important to me. . . ." (*Margaret* 6/93)

It was the nature of the relationships between the facilitators and Academy members that was most critical to the significant personal and professional growth experienced by many. Interactions were different depending on any number of factors. Although the role of the facilitator varied from person to person, the underlying intent—to devote a person's time exclusively to supporting school leaders' professional growth—never waivered in importance.

# MARKING LEADERSHIP GROWTH
## How I Affected My School

> The biggest stride for me was in confronting teachers about their behaviors, ones that have a negative impact on kids. I found out I could do it.
>
> *Fran 6/93*

Evaluating the outcomes of leadership development experiences has been as problematic down through the years as has evaluating the impacts of leadership itself. Uncertainties about what leadership looks like and how to measure its effects have given leadership evaluation a smoke-and-mirrors character. The members and staff of the Maine Academy became well acquainted with this quality of the assessment process.

The Academy courageously asserted that the leadership growth of its members would be measured in student outcomes. But how was this to occur? What leadership changes would members undertake? How would they eventually affect the learning of students? How long would such effects take to show up in student performance, behavior, and attitudes? Was it even possible to see any in the 16 months of the Academy?

The MASL program itself complicated the task. We dictated neither a uniform set of student outcomes members were to strive for nor the leadership processes members were to adopt. Quite to the contrary. We invited our members to invent their own more effective ways of influencing student learning according to the needs of their own schools. All parts of the program led toward the goal of assessing leadership in "student outcome" terms: the Leadership Development Plan, efforts of facilitators and S&D Teams, periodic written assessments using colleague feedback, and finally the Portfolio and Exhibition. In the final analysis, however, assessing each leader's impacts on students was the responsibility of the leader her- or himself.

By May and June of 1993, most members had made repeated attempts to gauge their effects on students. But by then these efforts were complicated by the fact that their LDPs had grown to include not only programmatic goals for student learning but interpersonal goals for affecting the colleagues who work with those students and intrapersonal goals for increasing knowledge of themselves as leaders. The I-C-I leadership model had propelled members to seek three simultaneous effects: (a) greater self-knowledge that would lead to (b) improved interpersonal behaviors with others at work so they, in turn, would (c) produce better conditions for learning among students. Measuring effects, then, meant evaluating not only how student learning may have changed but also how colleagues and the leader her- or himself may have changed.

Chapters 7 and 8 report the evidence of members' leadership growth in these three arenas. This chapter describes effects "outside" the leader on colleagues and on student outcomes. Chapter 8 looks at the origins of these in leaders' progress toward greater self-knowledge and self-improvement. Although evidence of change appears in all three arenas, it was in the third and personal arena of growth that many members came to see the greatest progress.

Source materials for these chapters were the external evaluation of the Academy, the written work of members, and observations by staff. The external evaluation drew from observation at Academy events, repeated surveys of members, and case studies of 14 diverse members (Johnson et al., 1993). It relied heavily on member reports. When taken together with the extensive documents collected by staff (journal entries, drafts of LDPs, periodic "taking stock" evaluations, and the final portfolio), the entire evaluation database is clearly subjective and weighted by member perceptions. To partially offset natural biases, we required members to include in their self-evaluations feedback on their leadership behaviors from colleagues at work and from the MASL facilitator and S&D Team members who observed in their schools. Some provided audio and video documentation of their leadership as well. MASL's guideline document for the self-assessment process, "Assessing Leadership Improvement," can be found in the Appendix.

## The External Evaluators' Summary

The Margaret Chase Smith Center for Public Policy at the University of Maine conducted the external evaluation of the Academy. Their report, "Program Evaluation: Maine Academy for School Leaders" (Johnson et al., 1993), described changes largely in two arenas: in leaders' attitudes, beliefs, confidence, and understanding of leadership; and in their behaviors with colleagues at school. They summarized the Academy's outcomes as follows:

> The participants believe that through the Academy's efforts they have had many significant learnings and have acquired skills which they have been able to apply at their sites for the benefit of all learners—students, teachers, administration, and staff. . . . Participants expanded their knowledge of interpersonal collaboration, group facilitation, leadership toward school improvement, and theories of leadership and educational change. They developed a greater capacity for evaluating staff-school conditions and their impacts on student outcomes. They are more able to develop practical and effective leadership strategies and to monitor their own success at employing those strategies. (p. 73)

Importantly, the team found much more evidence of conceptual and philosophical change and of the adoption of new interpersonal strategies than they did of improved student outcomes. The evaluation survey found that members focused during the Academy most on "how you act with colleagues at work" and on "specific behaviors to improve your leadership" and least on "specific student outcomes" (p. 47). The evaluation includes a number of self-reports by members on their impacts on students but these, like the ones later in this chapter, nearly always portray these student effects as vague and indirect or too far off in the future to document. They are usually clearer and more concrete about effects on colleagues. Here is an example from the report's Appendix H:

> My specific LDP assessment has had specific student outcomes (portfolio building for each child at each grade level, etc.). Beyond that, however, I have been encouraged by my headmaster to share [my strategies for using portfolios] with the middle school and upper school faculty. This has just recently begun to be accepted and to receive enthusiastic support and interest by these faculties. I hope that student outcomes will soon follow at these levels.

The evaluation report found that, first and foremost, MASL enabled most members to learn a great deal about leadership and themselves; only secondarily was it a concerted effort to change student learning in schools. Again, from the summary, the evaluation team wrote,

> The Academy encouraged participants to consider exploring, creating, and committing to a philosophy and approach [to leadership] rather than pressing for compliance to a predetermined and inflexible agenda [for school change.] The participants responded with a commitment to a process of learning and leadership development. They assumed ownership of the Academy's implementation and outcomes along with the [Academy's] leadership. Consequently, participants have greater self-awareness and are more oriented toward ongoing and self-directed personal and professional growth. (p. 73)

The program evaluation established that these positive aspects of the Academy reached all but a few of the 58 participants, concluding that collectively it had developed a "community of leaders" able to sustain and support one anothers' attempts at improvement. The team was unable to collect data on effects on student learning in part because they did not exist and in part because of logistical strictures. MASL attempted to address the need for such data by placing the burden of proof that such change was occurring on the leaders themselves. The remainder of this chapter is devoted to their words and their descriptions of change. We start with their assessments of their impacts on colleagues, then move to their impacts on students.

## Impacts on My Work With Adults

The interpersonal goals in members' LDPs addressed various specific strategies for working more effectively with colleagues, employees, parents, supervisors, school board members, and citizens in the interests of improving student outcomes. MASL's periodic "taking stock" self-evaluations and the final portfolio/exhibition process required members to collect and evaluate evidence that they had influenced these adults. Staff stressed the importance to this effort of direct feedback from the adults themselves.

Members' reflective and evaluative writings were rich with struggles to ascertain their new interpersonal effectiveness. In our reviews of these writings, we identified three major types of progress:

- Asserting a new leadership style with others
- Building a more productive relationship with others
- Opening up as a leader

This section of the chapter will illustrate each of these themes with a sample of excerpts from members' writings.

### *Asserting a New Leadership Style With Others*

Principals and teacher leaders alike came to the Academy with ambitions to lead in nontraditional ways. They hoped to empower colleagues, to form community leadership, to share responsibility for major decisions with those who would be influenced by them. Many LDP goals revolved around using consultative behaviors with adults and involving adults in solving their own problems. In their efforts to operationalize these, however, most members ran headlong into those adults' expectations—expectations framed and fueled by traditional structures and comfortable cultures.

Members' initial efforts to assert new leadership behaviors failed because, as one teacher put it, "[My colleagues] aren't ready for me to act this way." Other adults at school expected—and often seemed to want—their principals or lead teachers to continue to "be themselves." Successive efforts to change, then, aimed at gradually unfreezing the old role expectation and asserting a new one. Many found that they could succeed at this by first explaining their new approach, then using it. Ed, for example, worried about being seen as a "do nothing" principal when he decided to shift his style to escape his old "do everything principal" mantle:

> This might not seem like much, but it is a big thing for me. Perhaps the reality of the impossibility of the job expectations and my faith and confidence in my staff has finally given me enough confidence in myself to allow them the opportunity to take the lead. I have found that, while this at times puts me in the position of a seeming "do nothing," results have been very satisfactory.
>
> A case in point. We've been wrestling with issues surrounding decisions that were made at staff meetings being undermined and reversed in the hallways and parking lot by those who "didn't want to be the wet blanket" and speak up against the issue [in the meetings]. The teachers' association president discussed this with me as a concern about at least one other teacher who she saw as being primarily responsible for it and I agreed to raise the issue.
>
> Rather than say something inspirational like, "Let's not do this anymore," and expecting it to happen [as was my custom], we discussed the issue and spent a lot of time getting into the whys of it. In a nonthreatening way, I think, I fostered a discussion that wound up with a solution that addressed the needs of all staff members and was not devised by me. . . . We were able to work like a staff to resolve the problem. (*Ed* 12/92)

Like Ed, many members worried that a small step would not accomplish much and that, in fact, it could hurt them because any new behavior might be seen as not leading. But they found that if that step involved a specific behavioral change in a common staff setting, if it was explained, and if it was aimed at a productive purpose, major changes could result.

Principals often had to begin changing by restraining themselves from old habits and resisting patterns of behavior that colleagues, parents, and students had come to expect. In her final portfolio, for example, Tamara "owned up" to how her "Mrs. Fix-It" behavior patterns made staff too dependent on her:

> This style of leadership allows for no individual growth. The harsh reality is that this type of leader, though well intended,

provides no opportunity for teachers to acquire skills necessary to improve their self-worth and personal capabilities. Their involvement in conflict resolution is practically nil. The atmosphere remains stable and supportive but clearly at the emotional expense of the leader. In such an environment, teachers are still adolescents with a caretaker providing for them. I need to end the Mrs. Fix-It principal. (*Tamara* 1/93)

Principals then had to concentrate on appropriate replacement behavior. Tamara explained how she took one productive step to assert a "new image" to her staff:

As my examination and exploration continued, a new image began to emerge; the kind of leader Heifitz and Sinder identified: "A leader becomes a guide, interpreter, and stimulus of engagement. A leader's vision is the grain of sand in the oyster, not the pearl." As a grain of sand, my examination caused friction. Status quo was being challenged. Leadership at Shoreline School now required participation of more than just the designated leader. . . . [With the help of two MASL staff and a conference I attended, I worked on strategies to change this.]

I put my newly developed strategies to work at a teachers' meeting. Several teachers had come to me with the issue of offensive language in the teachers' room. They hoped I would address this with certain members of our staff. I instead placed it on the agenda for our next meeting. I brought the issue up and offered time for collaborative discourse. I gave no solutions, no fix-it strategies and no opinion.

An intense discussion ensued. Teachers felt empowered to share openly their differing opinions in a safe atmosphere. One teacher previously unable to address interpersonal conflicts expressed that she now felt able to confront offensive language with individuals when necessary. No longer did I need to step in as mediator, peace negotiator, or conflict manager.

I saw in my growth the growth of the staff. I learned that coloring the issues with my opinion did nothing but create an insistence of "please the principal." Now I realized that it was my role to open the doors of communication, not to be the sole communicator and fixer.

The role of caretaker was D for DONE. (*Tamara* 5/93)

A major challenge for many principals (and some teacher leaders) was to break old "take charge" habits traditionally associated with their roles. These tended to come into play almost involuntarily when they were confronted by a staff member or parent or a situation that was spinning out of control. At least half the Academy members included this syndrome in their goals for behavioral change. One administrator, after recounting a teacher's "attack" on her administration, described her behavioral shift this way:

> What was really so valuable for me [as this happened] was Covey's principle: "Seek first to understand, then to be understood" that I learned through the Academy. When I was being attacked by the teacher, I kept saying to myself, "Wait, I'm going to process this." In the whole situation, it was Leadership Academy going through my head [and it worked]. (*Faith* 6/93)

Another principal reported that she "learned to ask: 'Why are they doing this [to me] now?' and not to respond [when she felt attacked]. In many cases, situations like this came out all right, simply by waiting and asking myself, 'What is it they're doing this for?' [and putting the problem back where it belonged]." (*Doreen* 6/93)

In contrast to principals' new and less directive leadership styles, teacher leaders often strived simply to establish a leadership style that they felt was effective. Most teacher leaders wanted to be more influential in their schools but without appearing to seek power over colleagues or their principals. This was a delicate feat and one which most teacher leaders only began to accomplish. Tess, a secondary school department head, made strides in this respect on a committee to explore assessment:

> I would say that I have—because of my LDP—been more willing to direct things in a fairly subtle organizational way so that the process of investigation of the assessment of reading—the basis of our grant committee's work—can continue. What I mean is I make decisions and record our findings and future plans through the minutes I produce after each meeting so that we all know what we are doing, why we are doing it, and when we are going to do it.
>
> I do not direct very forcefully at all in the meetings themselves. I do not need to nor would it be appropriate. I think the

other teachers appreciate the kinds of organizing and communicating that I do and, in many ways, it makes them more committed and knowledgeable participants.

Because we are colleagues—rather than supervisor/employee—they do not mind as much, I think, the kind of organizing and managing I do. In fact, I like to think that they function so well because of the support I provide that they almost do not realize it. . . . (*Tess* 5/93)

Tess shared with most other teacher leaders the paradoxical goals of trying to be more direct in her influence in a way that "they almost do not realize." Teachers often accomplished this by being very active between meetings, conferring with colleagues, preparing written materials on behalf of the group, and advocating with administration.

Teacher leaders also increased their influence among their colleagues by consciously applying group facilitation techniques and concepts from the Academy. MASL's curriculum introduced members to team building and effective group performance practices; staff modeled these and encouraged S&D Teams to employ them. Some members built useful group techniques into the interpersonal strategies of their LDPs. Kim's portfolio documented how she used "authentic listening skills" with a "difficult member" on her grade-level team to clarify communication and reduce friction within the entire team. She was then able to help

my team discuss how we function as a team. I've given them some of the forms given to us by the Academy but *none* want a form. They want honest conversation. . . .

We have planned to set aside time before school closes to discuss how we function as a team. Here are some of the topics we'll be discussing: common planning time, the productivity of meetings, and being aware of feelings. Is each team member satisfied with the way things work? This is part of my plan for the future.

The most important issue we continue to struggle with is to put "housework" aside and to talk about children. I have learned that I will never please everyone but keeping communication open and not taking criticism personally is very healthy. (*Kim* 5/93)

MASL leaders were, for the most part, successful at taking such initial steps at redefining their operating styles as leaders. They found that they could succeed if they accounted for others' expectations, tried to explain their new approach, and introduced discrete new behaviors at appropriate times. By defining concrete behavioral shifts with specific people such as Kim's difficult team member or specific instances such as Ed's faculty meeting, they found they could begin the process of shifting relationships—and then staff behaviors—on a grander level.

## Building More Productive Relationships

The second impact many members felt they had on other adults grew from their success at shifting their leadership styles or roles. Once they had "unfrozen" the old patterns of behavior with others, they were able to build different working relationships with colleagues and among colleagues. In much the way Kim spoke of her ability to protect "honest conversation" among her teammates, others saw their behaviors eliminating static and hostility, focusing everyone's efforts "more on kids and less on politics," and generally raising the "authenticity" level among adults at school.

For some, creating trust and openness among teachers and between principal and teachers was a superordinate goal. Without these, they felt, no school could move forward as a unit and make learning more effective for kids. Ozzie, an elementary principal, made this happen by being open and honest himself:

> [My goal was] to establish a "climate of honesty" among staff. I need to deal openly and honestly with teachers and staff, especially when I have to be critical of some aspect of job performance.
>
> One of my proudest accomplishments at Sterling has been to instill a sense of openness and honesty at the school. Before my arrival, there was a great deal of mistrust. The teachers did not have much respect for the [principal], nor for some of their colleagues. There was much bickering, and morale was low.
>
> I have insisted that people take their complaints to the right source, and deal honestly with each other. The ultimate test of our "climate of honesty" came last June when I let go one of the teachers. I urged the teachers to keep their feelings out in the open and not to deal with any concern, anger, or frustration by

going underground. We came through this ordeal in a healthy manner. (*Ozzie* 5/93)

One of the most effective ways members found to establish new working relationships was to share their LDPs with colleagues and enlist them in giving feedback on their progress. This practice, although it took extraordinary courage at the start, nearly always led to strengthened relationships with colleagues and new levels of authenticity among colleagues. Here, Irene describes how she had strengthened her relationship with her staff:

I also received feedback from a faculty member [just recently]. This faculty member . . . and I have a long history of unfortunate comments and misunderstandings. That history made his comments so much more significant, both personally and professionally.

He unexpectedly appeared at my office door last Tuesday and asked if I had a minute. He proceeded to tell me how comfortable he was feeling with our working relationship this year. He knew that I was working hard to change some behaviors and improving some interpersonal relationships at school and that the hard work was paying off. He felt like the faculty had really pulled together and how much more comfortable people seemed to be with each other.

He cited the staff leadership team meeting from the day when teacher leaders and administrators took different sides on a topic. He stated, "It's okay for people to disagree with you and you to disagree with them." His next statements were interesting. He said, "I think you have taken the heat for a lot of things that are happening in this school that WE know are positive and significant changes, but that parents and community perceive as negative and wrong. I just wish that the community would be more patient with schools that are truly changing. We have a really good school and are doing lots of things for kids."

He concluded his visit by saying that he thought I had really grown into the job as principal and that he was supportive of me and just wanted me to know where he stood.

He could have knocked me over with a feather! (*Irene* 1/93)

Rather than attempting to change relationships with the whole staff at once, Irene and most others found greater success in changing how they worked with one person at a time. Some principals sought to clear the air with teachers, janitors, and other staff who had become thorns in their sides. Their LDPs focused on conflict management or helping others to see how their behavior was affecting people deleteriously. By working through strategies for confronting differences and past offenses, these members gradually began to shift their relationships with their entire staffs. Much to their surprise, they found that, as one principal put it, "once I started [acting this way with people] it was difficult to stop. *All* my relationships seemed to change!" (*Nathan* 12/92).

A surprising number of members sought to shift relationships with their bosses. Many of these were teacher leaders who saw, as part of their desire to influence the school more positively, that their relationships with principals would need to change. A high school teacher, for example, realized she had become "hypercritical" of her principal, blaming many of the school's ills and her own sense of powerlessness on the principal. The Academy helped Natalie to confront her own responsibility for this situation, which led her to seek out the principal and to initiate a forthright conversation with her about their relationship and how it was impairing Natalie's (and the principal's) effectiveness in the school. Their conversation cleared the air and made Natalie feel immensely more optimistic about her own ability to shape the school's affairs. Others addressed similar issues of trust, communication, and purpose with their superintendents and emerged feeling they had advanced the cause of student learning and strengthened their working relationships.

A few brave souls focused neither on changing relationships with individuals nor with their faculties but, instead, attempted to become new players on a districtwide stage. As difficult as this was, a couple of MASL leaders made progress on this front mostly through persistence, courage, and learning how to seize opportunities to define agendas and build coalitions. In one district, Cicely, an elementary teacher, was able to "step out of ranks" to help start an important curriculum council:

> In my gut, I knew I rubbed [some] people the wrong way, but I also knew my purpose was not self-promotion but improvement in "the way we do things around here." . . .
>
> Stepping out from the rank and file is a tremendous risk, one often viewed with suspicion and fraught with ostracism. At this

point, I was sorely aware of my shortcomings and yet fired up about the way things "could" be around our district. To bolster my courage and resolve, I practiced scripting my thoughts and presentations. . . .

As a leader, I hoped to provide a forum in which ideas, complaints, alternatives could be discussed and acted upon in a way that would help us rise above the perpetual grousing, back-stabbing, and suspicious nature of our ways. . . . I believe thinking through my own *agenda* and garnering support before the meeting were essential for the meeting's success. The following day, I wrote a note to members of the organizing team (key players, *not* the influential friends who received personal thanks). These are significant changes in the way I communicate with coworkers and higher-ups. . . .

The most courageous aspect of my LDP, to date, was calling the meeting to discuss curriculum coordination in the district. . . . Working toward a change in curriculum coordination would be uplifting the school culture, addressing the leadership challenge of my LDP, and providing a better coordinated learning environment for our students.

[But] calling the meeting was stepping out of ranks. I was careful to discuss the idea with higher-ups. Some greeted the idea with skepticism, others with polite, positive professionalism. . . . [In the meeting,] I worked hard to temper my zeal, to provide opportunities for discussion, to listen to others. *Mark this growth!* (*Cicely* 5/93)

## Opening Up as a Leader

Cicely's account of "stepping out" provides a vivid bridge to the third type of interpersonal impact that the Academy had. For many members, MASL nurtured the development of professional— and often personal—openness with colleagues, parents, bosses, and employees. Members drew from the Academy both new confidence in their own visions for their schools and a new interpersonal capacity for authentic communication. These combined to make them feel both more comfortable with others' beliefs and evaluations of school matters and freer to voice their own. The new relationships that began to form with other adults often made MASL leaders feel more comfortable in their leadership work.

For many, this kind of progress started with an "aha" about themselves and grew to a deeper understanding of the differences between their own and their colleagues' personal styles and professional beliefs. Eleanor, a middle-level team leader, illustrates this evolution:

> [After focusing entirely on clarifying my cognitive goals for the school] I slowly started to change the focus of my LDP to the interpersonal. I realized that I needed to improve a lot in my communications with people. Through working with the middle-level team, I found that it wasn't as easy as I thought to lead a group, even though I did think I had the skills to do it. . . . I've never focused on any kind of interpersonal skills in my career.
>
> We were learning a lot of communication skills [in MASL], how to relate to other people and to deal with conflict, how to listen effectively, etc., and I could see that I had made a lot of mistakes as a "leader" by not listening and by assuming that I was always right (which is a very hard notion to shake). . . .
>
> One of the most powerful MASL activities for me was the Myers-Briggs [Personality Type Inventory] analysis. . . . Suddenly I was faced with the reality that most people don't think like I do! . . . I thought this was amazing. This knowledge definitely toned down my relentless persistence that schools must change immediately to be the way that I want them to be.
>
> I still feel they need to change and I do feel that more and more people agree that they need to change but maybe all the changes that I would choose to make aren't going to work for everyone. . . . We are all different and I should not expect people to always come around to my way of thinking. (*Eleanor* 5/93)

These realizations made way for Eleanor and others to state more openly their own views and to respect and accommodate others'.

Commonly, as members' appreciation for personal differences grew, their behaviors with others—and especially colleagues and parents who had been obstacles to them—became more attentive, appreciative, and diversified. They, to a person, found that doing these things led to their being heard more clearly and, in the long run, having a more influential hand at work. Nina wrote,

I am in a constant (well, almost constant) state of perpetual reflection, thinking about recent interactions with others, running through the mental checklist of: don't be judgmental, listen carefully to what that person has to say, think before speaking, work on composing clearly articulated sentences, say what you mean. . . .

I have been prone to making snap decisions and shutting people out because I don't agree with what they're saying, because they have an abrasive style, because they don't look at me, because they're extraordinarily defensive, etc. Since acknowledging that behavior, I have found myself consciously trying to separate people's ideas from their styles. . . .

As a result of practicing nonjudgmental behavior, I am a better listener. I am a more constructive participant in meetings. People tend to listen more to what I say. I am a clearer thinker. I am a better leader. (*Nina* 5/93)

Listening better to others, ironically, made many members feel freer to voice their own thoughts to others. Especially for principals, the goal of *sharing* ideas, information, and decisions with others gradually infused their interchanges with staff and parents, replacing their old belief that they needed to *deliver* answers, directives, and solutions. This, in turn, unblocked the path to express more clearly and freely their beliefs and values for the school. Connie, an assistant principal, discovered that contrary to her assumption the faculty in her secondary school wanted direction from her and her principal. She understood this only after successfully establishing a relationship with them based on open, uncritical communication:

The other area where I have evidence of a slight success is in helping the principal develop a shared vision, mission, and values for the school. Through committee work and other meetings, I have had many opportunities to hear staff and express my value system. I have also sent out educational articles supporting my beliefs. As a result, faculty members have come to me to discuss the ideas and their ideas and to either agree or disagree with the thoughts presented.

I have found that the [our school's] people certainly like direction. They want to know, "Where are we headed?" Being clear about where I am going and why and having this direction built around my personal value system not only helps me but helps the faculty and staff as well. But I am not sure that until I did my LDP I knew exactly where I was headed or how I was going to get there. (*Connie* 12/92)

Other principals learned to be more forthright with teachers about issues of performance. Like principals everywhere, MASL principals felt caught between their desire to support teachers and build a strong collaborative team and their obligation to evaluate and take action about staff performance. Through interpersonal skills development and clarification of beliefs and standards, several found ways to take action with staff who were not working to their expectations. Much to their surprise, these encounters almost always were rewarded by both better relationships and better performance. In some, they led to the appropriate removal of a substandard employee. Fran, for example, shared this reflection on how she benefited from the Academy:

I learned more about myself than I ever have. From my S&D Team, especially. They helped me confront who I was and when I was pulling one of my avoidance things. . . . Through David Sanderson's modeling [at Bowdoin], I saw how he addressed his own responsibility for a situation with the group and dissected it as an honest person. He confronted it and helped the group confront it. Many times this year, I did the same thing at work because of that.

The biggest stride for me was in confronting teachers about their behaviors, ones that have a negative impact on kids. I found out I could do it. . . . I just had to be direct with [a teacher], express how it concerned me and how I believed it was hurting kids. He cried . . . and his classroom changed *immediately*. . . .

Getting the guts came from the Academy: I got rid of a counselor; the secretary is gone; and this teacher has changed. Confronting their behaviors and knowing I'd get through it was the key. (*Fran* 6/93)

Opening up with others put MASL leaders' relationships at work on a new plane. On one hand, they were more interpersonally sensitive to the fact that colleagues, employees, and parents viewed their work differently. On the other, this knowledge permitted them to articulate more directly their own views and to give others the opportunity for dialogue.

## Impacts on Student Outcomes

Evaluating how members' leadership behaviors were affecting student learning was, without question, a daunting task. As one member put it, "I'm overwhelmed with trying to change how I'm leading and now you're asking me to document how it's affecting kids. Hold on!" (*Bill* 10/92). MASL staff, although acknowledging how ambitious this goal was, reminded, encouraged, coached, and cajoled members throughout the Academy to keep running records of their effects on kids, however remote they may be. The final portfolios included the evidence they collected. They reported three major types of student effects:

- Direct effects on students a member worked with
- Simultaneous effects of working with staff and students
- Indirect effects of advocacy for students and student programs

### Direct Effects

Direct effects were most frequently documented by teacher leaders. They often blurred teachers' teaching and leadership roles and built on the concept of the leader as a "head learner." For example, Barbara, a high school English teacher, articulated her impacts by listing how she had used new group discussion and learning techniques experienced in MASL in her classes to help her students learn English. She also described how she had been able to get students to "take more risks" in publishing their writing and attending the Bread Loaf Young Writers' Conference at Middlebury College. She drew a direct connection between her own learning about her role as a lead teacher and her new approach to working with students: "Facilitating those kinds of learning experiences is, for me, the culmination of my own learning. If others had not facilitated my learning and encouraged me to be patient with ambiguity, to take risks, to reflect on practice, my students would not be perform-ing as they are" (*Barbara* 5/93).

Many members echoed the theme that MASL's greatest impact on students was through what they had learned about learning itself. They took experiences from their own learning in MASL, such as setting learning or behavioral goals or using portfolios, and put them to use with their students. In this vein, Charlotte, an eighth-grade team leader, wrote, "I've had my kids do a *lot* more self-evaluation not only of their products but also of the process of how they got to where they ended up" (*Charlotte* 5/93). Others described how they had students develop contracts for learning and how they organized exhibitions of learning for parents and students.

Some leaders took from the Academy a clearer philosophy and specific practices to help their students take more responsibility for their own learning. Here, Orin (an elementary school teacher leader) describes how his sharing of his own learning experiences served as a public model for his students and coteacher:

> Early in the year, I involved the students in a discussion that has also helped to shape our year in a more positive way. Both as a reminder to me but also as a way of broadening the students' perspectives, I made a sign listing my strengths and weaknesses. I made a real effort to connect the strengths with corresponding weaknesses, thereby suggesting that if we have a fault it should not make us feel horrible, but that it is part of a larger self full of strengths and weaknesses.
>
> The kids have responded well, and I think the discussion laid in place an important theme that we have revisited much this year: The most important part of learning is figuring out where we are and working to get to the next level. I have also used the poster in disciplinary situations, pointing out to people that their disruptive behavior is probably linked to a strength and that they should focus on how to build on that part while trying to control the negative. The poster has kept me focused on one very impor-tant part of my LDP. (*Orin* 5/93)

Ceilah, a high school English department chair, made a correspond-ing connection between her own learning in MASL and the sorts of things she was doing in her classroom and encouraging among her English department colleagues:

The place where there's the greatest chance of impact on kids is in portfolio development. As a classroom teacher, I've learned a lot about dealing with broad expectations. It may be freeing in some ways, but it has incredible responsibility with it. . . . It made me realize how difficult this thing of school reform is. We are in cooperative learning workshops [at school] this week and I see [my colleagues] learning *about* it, but not *doing* it. We *did* it in MASL. . . .

Building in time for reflection is so important [to such efforts]. MASL's allowed me to do that and I realize how important this is for kids. I'm going to ask everyone in the department next year to find ways to get kids to reflect on what they learn and how to assess it. (*Ceilah* 5/93)

And for some, their work with children—either in academic instruction or in personal development—changed because they learned something about themselves and how they work with others. Tanya wrote,

The Academy has helped me observe better, not jump in right off. And this has given me more confidence. . . . When you know who you are, you relax a little; so to relating to children, I'm not dealing with my own issues any more . . . I'm not doubting myself . . . I've learned to step back. (*Tanya* 6/93)

And Bill, a middle school teacher, reported,

I feel so much better about my work with eighth graders because I took the time in the Academy to look at me and how I was growing and to figure out how I was communicating that to kids. I began seeing those 42 eighth graders as learners in the same way I was a learner. My job was to meet their needs, their growth. Without MASL, I'd still be looking for more tricks for my bag of tricks.

[I've realized that I've learned a lot] about student ownership for their education. That's what MASL did for us. I see us doing the same for our kids. . . . I've been working to make myself, then others, more responsible for their own learning and own future. (*Bill* 6/93)

These descriptions of members' direct impacts on students are encouraging but problematic. They indicate that the Academy permitted some members to make significant changes in their work with students. At the same time, however, they do not document effects on student outcomes and, notably, they are limited largely to teacher leaders and their work within their own classrooms.

### Simultaneous Effects on Staff and Students

A second and more common way that members described their impacts on student learning was through their leadership of a staff group or an individual in matters that had a direct bearing on a student or a group of students. Their LDPs specified new leadership behaviors to apply as they worked to change interpersonal patterns among adults to improve student learning for a specific student or group. For these leaders (and we suspect for most leaders), impacts on colleagues and on students were simultaneous and inseparable.

One way members saw themselves affecting student learning was by enabling the faculty team to have greater responsibility for and control over student outcomes. Many Academy members' LDPs centered on enlisting colleagues to identify student outcome goals, develop new practices with and for students, and evaluate student gains. The upshot often was more widespread ownership for student learning among faculty. Delany, an elementary assistant principal, described this evolution and its impacts on students this way:

> I had originally planned in my LDP "to develop a program for at-risk students," which I did. But this program is ongoing and expanding even as I speak. The staff had originally wanted a room to place all the hard kids in so "they could get the help they needed." (This was where my new interpersonal focus on sharing problem solving with the staff came in.) Through creating times to look at those students and to talk about those students, the staff now realizes that *they* are the help those kids need.
>
> The staff is looking at what they do for students and what help they need to do their jobs better. We have met in groups to talk about students and had people come in to talk to us about students. We have developed before- and after-school programs to meet some of the needs. We have developed a one-on-one

connection with certain adults and certain children for specific reasons to meet student needs. We have developed a network of support systems that we can access.

The evidence I will look for [to evaluate our success in the future] will be the same as what I looked for this year. I would hope to see more decisions being made based on what is best for the students and what is best for the students will be based on what the students are learning. (*Delany* 5/93)

Many leaders found that their efforts to involve teachers in planning and decision making focused staff time more on student issues. For example, Harris "stopped trying to get staff to deal with petty things" and did them himself. When he did, he found his faculty taking on "more conceptual and programmatic things like assessment, test scores, and portfolios" (*Harris* 6/93). Similarly, Nathan, who was the principal in Charlotte's junior high, commented that "Charlotte's leadership of the eighth-grade team had a big impact on kids in our building. Her leadership, reinforced by her LDP and us, brought the team from a daily bitch session to a meeting that could make decisions about kids" (*Nathan* 6/93). Charlotte herself reported that

being more organized let our team focus on kids more. I looked back at our agendas and saw how much more *kids* were on our agendas. And there were a couple of units we did as a group. Then we evaluated how things went with kids a lot more. We were paying attention to the fact that planning and evaluation are important. (*Charlotte* 6/93)

A number of members' LDPs concentrated on new interpersonal skills with staff that would focus attention more on students and less on what one leader called "off-task behavior." Belle, a high school assistant principal, worked on "meeting skills" and specifically on setting up and supporting "year-long research and open discussion groups" to focus on student learning issues. Then, she applied her skills in a series of faculty meetings to review, evaluate, and make decisions about the results of these research groups. In May 1993, she wrote,

The integrated learning research spawned the applied physics course that took place in the shop. . . . Two other interdisciplinary classes emerged—American studies that combined art, music,

American literature, and history; and architectural drafting that combined art and drafting with a new CAD system. . . . (*Charlotte* 5/93)

Most Academy members were able to document ways that their work with staff had thrust a particular program, student outcome, or new teaching practice onto the staff agenda. Many could point to a specific change in practice or policy. Although they could not produce the student outcome "proof" for these changes, they often were convinced that their leadership eventually made enough difference to yield such proof.

### Indirect Effects

Members reported a third impact on student learning: indirect effects through their increased ability to advocate for students and learning issues in their schools and districts. They documented, often convincingly, how their LDP activities had placed them in positions and situations in which their student outcome focus was spread to others or written into decisions, programs, and policies. Although no student effects were documented, these leaders' successful efforts to get the ball rolling toward such effects were often corroborated by colleagues at work, by S&D Team members, and through the observations of MASL facilitators.

Teacher leaders most graphically demonstrated this kind of growth. Because they were more likely not to have legitimate standing as leaders at the outset of the Academy, the development of their advocacy for student learning was significant. One elementary teacher in a large city system, for example, devoted much of her LDP to becoming more self-confident and assertive on a district-wide assessment committee. At the Academy's close, she wrote,

> Our whole assessment system in Kingston changed this year and I was on that committee. The Assistant Superintendent told me I had a big effect on this outcome. Our committee blazed the trail [for a new testing and assessment system for every child]. And now I've been asked to chair the next [year's committee]. (*Shelly* 6/93)

Bonnie, a gifted and talented program coordinator also working on assertiveness skills, typified many teacher leaders. Her professional life had been devoted to being a good "team player," working hard to please her principals and the district. As she contemplated more active leadership, she found herself facing the choice between being compliant and speaking out for student interests. Unlike how she would have once acted, this time she stepped out:

> Last week I read in the newspaper that my program was canceled. I said to myself, "If I'm a leader, I'll [do something about this; it's my responsibility]." So I called the superintendent and didn't complain but said, "What can I do?"
>
> So I went to the board meeting and spoke about the cuts. I was encouraged by a board member to come. They agreed to wait until the Gifted and Talented Advisory Council could come up with some alternative programs . . . over the protestations of the superintendent and *all* the principals.
>
> The upshot was, now we're in a reduced mode. But we're still in existence! (*Bonnie* 6/93)

The LDP and the thought that went into its planning gave members a strategy for advancing agendas for students into the worklife of the school. Whether through making meetings more task-oriented, less overwhelmed by "petty stuff," or less conflictual, many reported success at getting colleagues and even their bosses to make decisions and take action around specific proposals for students. When the Academy ended, many of these proposals were reaching stride. A few were still experiencing start-up difficulties but MASL leaders felt they were influencing the course of events more directly. Cicely demonstrated the optimism, energy, and sense of efficacy that often accompanied this progress:

> This curriculum coordination committee is so exciting . . . and such a challenge. It's going! It's a whole new LDP!! It's teachers coming up with new ideas for programs. We've gotten financial support from the board! And these'll effect kids directly! It's a new model for our system! . . . (*Cicely* 6/93)

## Summary:
## We've Only Just Begun . . .

These descriptions by Academy members of their effects on colleagues and students are often short on hard evidence but long on confidence. Documentation is anecdotal and mostly from self-reports. Although it no doubt is suspect from the tough-minded evaluator's viewpoint, it nevertheless exudes a spirit of optimism that seems to bode well for the future impacts of these leaders' efforts. When viewed against the long evolution of these leaders' LDPs and of their self-concepts as leaders, the evidence of success they present seems more plausible. This is especially true when we remind ourselves of the short time span in which they worked.

In closing this first chapter on effects, we are reminded that most members themselves viewed their effects on colleagues and students as tentative and preliminary. They had just begun to thaw colleagues' established expectations of them as leaders. In May 1993, they were still establishing discrete new behaviors and asserting the hint of a new style. New behavior patterns were starting to change their relationships with colleagues, often one person at a time. As they became clearer about their styles, roles, and relationships, some members found themselves feeling more comfortable about express-ing beliefs and feelings with colleagues. In some cases, this heralded a new spirit and openness among the staff groups they led.

Effects on students were more difficult to identify, particularly for principals. Although teacher leaders could often point to new practices they had initiated in their own classrooms, it was harder for either teachers or principals to identify how they had influenced new practices in others' work with students. Most members de-scribed their impacts on students by finding in their work evidence that they were simultaneously affecting a specific student or group of students. Finally, some could point to the indirect effects they believed they had on students through specific actions they took to advocate for student programs and services.

We view these reports with the same tentative eye that our MASL colleagues used in writing their final portfolios. We do so in large part because of how ambitious it was to believe that any leadership growth could generate discernible student growth within a 16-month period. We recognize, as well, that some members made few persisting changes in their own behaviors, let alone in the behavior and learning of staff or students. As we turn in the next chapter to members' analysis of growth in their own learning, however, we find reason to be optimistic about their effectiveness over the long haul.

# MARKING LEADERSHIP GROWTH
## Seeing Changes in Myself

Do the intrapersonal changes I made have a direct impact on my students? In some ways, I feel they did. But it'll take more than 16 months to show. The biggest payoffs were to me.

*Ed 6/93*

Ed could have been speaking for most of his Academy colleagues. In the final analysis, the greatest changes that MASL leaders were able to identify from the Academy experience were changes within themselves, not among their colleagues or in student learning. Although the ultimate test of this professional growth lies in its impact on others and on the school's performance, change in leaders' beliefs, attitudes, self-perceptions, and formal knowledge can be said to underpin and precede impacts on others. Indeed, the I-C-I learning model stood on the premise that leaders build the capacities of others in their school communities by learning about and building their own capacities as people and as leaders.

By the Academy's end, nearly every MASL member's experience had reinforced this premise. With only rare exceptions, these leaders attested frequently and eloquently to the importance of intrapersonal learning to their leadership of others. Both the external evaluation of the Academy and staff observation confirmed the depth of these impacts. This chapter will illustrate four ways that many members felt they had changed through the MASL experience. They gained the following:

- Greater insight into what leadership demanded of them behaviorally, emotionally, and intellectually
- Greater insight into their qualities and challenges as leaders
- Greater confidence in themselves as leaders
- The ability to reflect on their actions and effects as leaders and, in turn, shape their effectiveness more purposefully

## Understanding the Demands of Leadership Better

Every MASL member found the Academy a rich opportunity to explore the concept of leadership in the very real contexts of his or her own school and his or her own self. This exploration uncapped a stream of questions about members' effectiveness as leaders. These, in turn, gave rise to more questions about what constituted effective leadership for their own schools. Pursuit of these questions alone and through S&D Team activities, facilitator consultation, writing, and Academy sessions helped members to understand better what leadership required of them on a personal level.

Most MASL members came to the Academy believing that leadership was largely a matter of "having the right ideas" and providing "answers and solutions" learned from courses, books, and experts. They left, however, understanding that successful leadership involved learning what others need from leaders and building what Irene called a common "accurate picture" of their work together:

One thing has become crystal clear to me: The cognitive component is my strength. I enjoy knowledge—acquiring it, manipulating it, and reforming it. I'm also more aware that I use this strength to cover up my weaknesses—and I do that very well. I knew that the interpersonal and intrapersonal components of leadership were the things getting me in difficult situations with faculty members, but I covered it up by intellectualizing. . . .

I knew I had plenty to learn but others expected me to have the answers. Over the past 12 to 14 months I have realized that

I have a very different picture of myself than do others. I don't have all of the answers! By sharing with my faculty the areas that I am trying to improve, by asking them for assistance with situations, by telling them my fears as a leader, the picture they have of me and the picture I have of me are coming closer together.

I think a successful leader is one where the pictures in everyone's heads are in focus and can be interchanged easily. For this to happen it requires time and energy. Everyone has to work on creating accurate pictures—but especially the leader. (*Irene* 5/93)

Listening to and watching their schools —and themselves at work in them—shifted MASL members away from largely rational and theoretical conceptions of leadership toward conceptions in which others' actions, feelings, and beliefs were considered vital influences. However unacceptable or different these might be to the leader, they learned to accept how important "where others are coming from" is to the leader's success at moving the school.

Acknowledging the sometimes messy realities of their schools and their colleagues helped many members gradually realize that there were no neat formulas or "silver bullets" for successful leadership. Improving themselves as leaders was not a matter of finding the "right stuff," adopting "effective leader" characteristics, or picking up specialized "tools." It began to look more like an interactive and interdependent "fitting" of themselves and the school's realities. Leading looked less like "doing to" and more like "doing with," less like applying formulas and policies and more like applying judgment and care. Barbara, a teacher leader, recognized this change in her thinking as she reflected on two early drafts of her LDP goals:

In my original application, I listed four goals for my continuing professional development:
1. Continue training in conflict resolution.
2. Continue training in developing inclusive curricula.
3. Research current theory and practice in evaluation.
4. Investigate models for inservice and ongoing professional education.

If one needs proof that the Academy has had an effect, if its I-C-I framework has changed our perspective, compare those to the goals I'd identified by April 1992:

1. Continue training in active listening.
2. Dull the edge on my acerbic sense of humor.
3. Share/delegate/let go of responsibility.
4. Work on a sense of perspective, seeing the glass as half full rather than half empty. (*Barbara* 5/93)

Barbara, like many of her MASL colleagues, incorporated interpersonal considerations into her second draft that were only remotely evident in her first. Her analysis of "people needs" at school has led her to identify some specific intrapersonal attributes such as her "acerbic sense of humor" as potential problem spots to work on.

Learning what their schools needed in a leader often propelled MASL members into a jungle of expectations, demands, legal requirements, and psychological and institutional needs. Their schools wanted everything from their leaders! A major challenge for members was the task of choosing *which* school needs they should devote their limited leadership energies to. They were pestered and even paralyzed by the worry that a focus on one set of needs would automatically preclude success with another set. Although our members discovered no formula for handling this age-old dilemma, many learned to make their own choices rather than continue to be buffeted by events and people into activities they found meaningless.

Members who seemed to make the greatest strides often chose to work on the toughest of their leadership tasks. These were usually challenges that members had avoided dealing with for months or even years, persisting issues that not only hurt the school but ate away at the leader, making her or him less effective in all aspects of his or her work. Thus some dealt with a long-standing conflict that was incapacitating a team or with a problematic staff member or boss. Others confronted their anxieties and insecurities in addressing public groups, running meetings, or developing consensus on important topics that divided the staff or staff and parents. Many concentrated on developing coherent "credos" or "personal mission" statements because they realized their scattered approaches to leading were leaving their colleagues uncertain and fragmented.

From this work, members came to understand that deciding what to do as a leader was a matter of listening more attentively both to their schools and to themselves. It especially meant confronting rather than ignoring or resisting the dilemmas that proved most personally troubling in this mix. Many credited our Bowdoin sessions with consultant Lucianne Carmichael for helping them confront this basic leadership principle. Abbie's description of Carmichael's impact was typical of many:

> My translation of [Lucianne's advice at Bowdoin] is slightly modified: Everyone has something to teach me. If I don't like someone, that is an indication of the differences between us. The greater the differences are, the more there is for me to learn. I only learn by listening carefully and sincerely. Therefore, if I don't like someone, I must make an effort to listen to him or her carefully, to ask the sorts of questions that elicit substantive answers, to recognize that this person provides a viewpoint that I need.
>
> The funny thing is that, after all of that, I often find that I like him or her. In fact, a focus of my LDP was to learn to handle conflict, but I've discovered that, by listening sincerely to different points of view, I've cut down on the everyday conflicts within the department.
>
> The other principle that I've incorporated into my leadership that helps here is Steven Covey's concept of "Win-Win or No Deal." If [our department] couldn't agree on an outcome, we kept working until we developed something that we all liked. No one could overrule anyone else.
>
> This synergy seems to have paid off. Just before Christmas, a member of my department came to me to ask for advice on a student with a serious reading problem. We talked it through and tracked down money to bring in a reading tutor twice a week. This encounter was doubly pleasing to me: It showed that this teacher, someone with whom I have not always worked well, trusted me enough to show that she had a problem; and it allowed me to provide the kind of leadership that I have aspired to, to find ways to help teachers to do what they know needs to be done. (*Abbie* 5/93)

Careful and prolonged analysis of the school's needs for leadership led, in this way, to listening to and watching oneself and how one did—or more often did not—seem to be meeting the school's needs. Many made a valuable discovery in this process: Their leadership behaviors and styles tended to favor what they saw as their strengths as educators and as people. For example, Tamara was terrific at stepping in and solving staff problems; Irene had a deep knowledge of teaching styles, curriculum, and research; and Bill was an extraordinary organizer and director of programs. Although the Academy and colleagues often encouraged these strengths, members' schools *always* needed more or different leadership than what these strong suits provided. It proved very difficult for many leaders to come to terms with the fact that their talents were not sufficient to meet all leadership demands. Again, Irene repeated advice from Lucianne Carmichael: "Once you figure out what your strengths are, you better find out where the delicate fulcrum is between enough and too much. . . . [A strength] can go too far. Caring is like that. It's a strength to care. Caring too much can be a weakness" (*Irene* 5/93). This discovery led members to whole new understandings of what their schools needed, understandings that were not limited by their own fears that they might not be able to provide for all those needs themselves.

As members saw their school environments more fully, they also came to understand more deeply how those environments were affecting them as leaders. Time, trial-and-error implementation of LDPs, and Academy support for reflection often brought members to see themselves as leaders who were not only "acting upon" others but who were, as well, "acted upon by" others. This discovery was for many a moment of profound insight, one that permitted them to act on those influences affecting their thoughts, feelings, and behaviors in ways they considered problematic. A vivid example of this "aha!" experience comes from Corinne, an elementary principal:

> Power and politics are a double reality in the life of a leader. In the June 1992 Bowdoin reflection, I stated: "Power is something most educators don't have and typically don't know how to access or utilize." I still believe this and now have concluded it is because most educators are women. Our culture has long held women as having roles "to make everything okay." Typically, women shy away from conflict. This leaves them with less skills than men in handling conflict. Elementary schools in particular have harbored the dominant father image of leadership.
>
> My interest in this concept grew out of a gender-specific episode of role-playing at Bowdoin. The Academy membership is made up primarily of women and "a few good men." The role-play happened to include three men and several women.

The men immediately formed a power base in the scenario we were acting out. They left out the other participants; I was strongly impacted because of the leadership role implicit in the role assigned to me.

The experience has served me well! I can identify this behavior more fully now. In July, I thought I had *never experienced* gender-specific issues around authority. In truth, I have learned that I *never recognized* them before. The role-play was "totally out in the open" so that all the interactions were clearly visible. I had just never seen and heard the entire play, scene by scene, including the reviews and the actors' responses to the reviews.

Now I recognize the play by just experiencing a part of a scene! . . . This knowledge has been *immensely* helpful to me within many of my leadership arenas. . . . (*Corinne* 5/93)

The development of insights like this was widespread in the Academy. In some respects, we see members' understanding of the dynamics of school leadership as the greatest outcome of the Academy. However, our purpose was to help these Maine leaders use these insights to shape their own behaviors so they could *act more successfully* as leaders within that dynamic. A second tier of insights, those dealing with themselves and *their suitedness to leadership,* often developed from this first tier. These brought MASL members a step closer to changing their own actions at work.

## Understanding How
## I Can Lead at My School

As members came to grips with specific leadership demands in their schools, MASL staff and S&D Team colleagues kept asking, "What does this mean for you? How can *you* fill these demands?" The intrapersonal dimension of the LDP became a place for members to wrestle with the answers to these questions. Many made important discoveries about themselves in the process, discoveries about how their personal qualities, habits, and skills affected their leadership.

This learning often affected leaders powerfully. It permitted them to create enduring, practical developmental goals. Most important, these were goals that these leaders, because they dealt first with themselves as individuals and not a wide array of other people, could control and work on. Nancy, a secondary teacher leader, provides an example of this:

> The final and perhaps the most important of my issues is my ability to differentiate between thinking aloud and presenting a new idea. I originally thought I needed to more clearly articulate my thoughts, but as I considered my Myers-Briggs type, it became apparent that my "E" [extrovert] trait was not clearly understood by all. I first realized that when I was rambling on in a meeting I finally came to the idea I really wanted to keep. I knew [to be understood as a leader] I had to indicate to people the difference between my thinking aloud and the idea I really wanted them to hear.
>
> I began to be more aware of when I was thinking and when my idea was crystallized. I now regularly notify listeners when I am thinking and when I am presenting a "real idea" I would like them to consider. This can be noted through my journals as well. This concept of clarifying my thoughts closely relates to expressing my needs, which has been an important issue for me as I have pondered where I wish to expend my energy and what role I might play beside the role(s) of teacher/teacher leader/association president. (*Nancy* 5/93)

Another teacher leader, Becky, illustrated in her portfolio two aspects of her leadership that she isolated for developmental work. She came to see her own development as a matter of behaving differently when she found herself in certain leadership situations at school. She called these in-action learning opportunities "learnable situations." Here are two of hers:

> 1. During a well-planned meeting when everything is going along well, a negative comment or angry outburst suddenly is heard. I am learning to pay attention to that . . . to set aside "my agenda" and hear that person out. I am also learning not to take it personally . . . to ask open questions that encourage the person to vent at the time, not hours or days later, or never.
>
> 2. I have learned to be more assertive and confront people to get to the bottom of an issue. I too often see people stew and fret

about a decision or some treatment rather than facing it head-on and clearing it up. In the above situation [in which the superintendent did not publicly support an exchange program which he had privately promised he would], I called the superintendent a few days after the board meeting and asked if I could meet with him. He came to my office after school that day, and we had a very honest discussion about what had happened. I told him exactly how I felt about it. I was calm but made it very clear to him how his lack of trust affected our working relationship.

I have done this more than once this year, and we are able to communicate quite clearly. Whether this communication is genuine beneath the surface remains to be seen. I'm sure there will be ample situations to find out! (*Becky* 5/93)

Through developing focused plans for improving leadership behaviors, a number of MASL members achieved a more realistic understanding of their strengths and weaknesses. From this understanding grew greater self-confidence as leaders. Self-assessment instruments, role-plays and observations, and reflective writing and consultation helped members see more clearly their own personal readiness to meet the challenges of their schools. One aspiring principal summarized her new knowledge this way:

Six months ago, I was going to be a principal. Three weeks ago, I turned down that opportunity. Six months ago I felt that I would be a dynamic school leader. Three weeks ago I said "not in this school." Six months ago I had the degrees, the motivation, and the drive. Three weeks ago, I had all of that and more.

The Academy has afforded me the luxury of getting to know me. It has forced me to look at who I am and how I operate. As a result, when what I thought was the golden opportunity [to move into a principalship] was placed before me, I had a new way to approach my decision.

Instead of looking at my needs, desires, and aspirations, I took time to look at my skills, strengths, and weaknesses. I based the decision on what I was capable of doing and what was needed and I realized that this was not a match. Six months ago, I would have applied for the job, and it would have been a mistake!

Learning to lead means knowing when to and when not to lead. It is a realization of what you are personally capable of doing and what you aren't. It is an honesty that only the "leader" knows of and must come from within. . . . It is knowing where your strengths will take you and how your weaknesses will haunt you. . . . (*Fran 8/92*)

Ceilah, a high school department chair, summarized well what many others experienced as they came to understand the importance of the "fit" between themselves and a leadership position:

It's been like Barth's title, *Improving Schools From Within.* What you did is work from within yourself and your group. It's what you do with what you've got now, not whether you have the ideal or not. Find out who you are first, then come up with what's appropriate for you [as a leader]. That's what's been so good about the Academy. (*Ceilah 6/93*)

Gaining this self-knowledge freed members from unrealistic and even impossible conceptions of leadership and expectations for themselves. Although many could document only their initial changes toward "fitting" themselves better to the leadership demands of their jobs, simply seeing their work in this manner was a major breakthrough.

## Gaining the Confidence That I Can Lead

The third common outcome documented by many MASL members was greater confidence in their leadership capacities. Such confidence often seemed an outgrowth of the clearer understanding of leadership and of their own "fit" with their positions noted in the first two sections. It showed up in members' writing and particularly in their reflections on specific leadership events. Many members wrote about "feeling so much better" about their roles and about "having my priorities straight" as a leader and person. But the biggest boost often came from the perception that adults at work were responding to them differently. Eleanor, a teacher leader, for example, wrote,

I can definitely say that people treat me differently [now than at the start of the Academy]. I feel more competent, more respected, more proud of my work. At the same time, I have definitely withdrawn from the "rat race" mentality [of trying to be all things to all people]. (*Eleanor* 12/92)

One way that members grew in self-confidence was through overcoming a long-standing hurdle and building on subsequent feelings of enhanced personal and professional efficacy. The LDP and the laborious process of targeting challenging goals frequently helped members take the first run at the hurdle. From there, success bred success. Deborah, for example, at first worried that her principal might try to restrict her efforts to "step out" as a leader. Once she summoned the courage to approach the principal and share her plans, however, she was surprised to find that her principal welcomed her and the initiative she wanted to take in school. From clearing this initial hurdle, Deborah learned that

> knowing that leadership comes from my own efforts, conversations, behaviors, and attitudes, while confronting at times, has actually freed me up to begin working for change in the school, instead of waiting for someone to create the perfect leadership role for me. I know I have a certain amount of power to change our school, through projects and other traditional roles, but also through being positive, communicating authentically, and sharing my learning with others. (*Deborah* 12/92)

It is noteworthy in Deborah's recounting of her growth that her LDP-driven actions changed *herself* more than they changed her principal. Members' increased sense of professional efficacy stemmed as much from removing internal obstacles as from removing external obstacles. The main ingredients in this process were a plan for behaving in a new way, support from colleagues both in MASL and at work, and the courage to take risks with others at work. The Academy was the staging area and the support system for most of these risks. Then, as they repeated new behaviors, new patterns eventually formed not only in their own behaviors but in the behaviors of those they interacted with at work. Connie, a secondary assistant principal, illustrated how success begot success and greater self-confidence:

> The first example of progress was my overall feeling. I began to feel more confident about what I had done. I trusted myself that I was handling the situation in the best way that I could. I did

not avoid these [difficult] individuals and when I met with them I left feeling that I had a better understanding of where they were coming from. I [worked hard] not to feel attacked and defensive or to feel the need to "make them happy."

As our relationship changed, we were communicating on a new level. They have proactive solutions to problems. One of them actually said to me, "I was proud of how you handled that rude parent." The positive comments, of course, are very enjoyable; however, the not-so-positive comments now are very helpful and solution-focused too: "I have an idea on how we could have handled that better."

It's far from perfect and I still have a way to go before this becomes second nature to me, but I am beginning to see those individuals in a different light, and I am conveying that to them. (*Connie* 12/92)

Some gained confidence initially by working through challenging experiences in Academy sessions, with their S&D Team members or facilitators. Here, the experiential learning model of the Academy provided a safer setting than school in which to try new behaviors with others. Harris, a seasoned elementary principal, credited his S&D Team's experiences with conflict and confrontation with showing him how he could confront challenging staff members at school:

MASL was the first time I had the opportunity as a professional to look at my *self*. All the courses I've taken and the Maine Principals' Academy previously had focused on the cognitive. This allowed me to look at *me* and to look at *others* in order to [see myself better], especially within my staff. . . .

I now find it easier to confront staff because of my S&D Team experience [in which we were able to confront each other and create a stronger, more honest team]. When you confront a person it's not an attack; it has to do with an issue, not with the person. Before, I'd avoid it—and then I'd get angry, then it would be an attack. Now I put more responsibility on others. (*Harris* 6/93)

For many principals, greater self-confidence grew from having others' assistance in identifying their strengths and weaknesses.

This external validation helped principals see themselves as their faculties saw them. MASL colleagues could also then assist them to prioritize how their talents and energies could best be deployed. Fran, for example, found that she needed to react less impulsively to others and to gain control over her own time and goals:

> I spend a lot of time thinking about my options, comments, and approaches and considering other peoples' styles, behaviors, and personalities, taking into account their possible concerns, comments, and needs.
>
> I have avoided crisis management as much as possible. I have become organized with my time and schedule that allows me to spend more time having conversations with people and being with kids.
>
> I have learned what my weaknesses are. I am *aware of them* and I work hard at compensating for them. (*Fran* 5/93)

For teacher leaders, building confidence often involved developing a sense of legitimacy for one's role in team or school affairs. This comes through in Deborah's previous description of meeting with her principal and discovering that the obstacles to her leadership were less with her principal than within herself. Ceilah, a secondary school department head, may have captured best the evolution of this sense of legitimacy as a leader. This evolution was the unifying theme of her final portfolio:

> [At the outset of the Academy,] I wasn't even sure if I belonged in this group [with these "real" leaders]. On another more instinctive level, though, I knew why I was there: I needed to become more confident in myself as a leader. It is interesting for me to look back at the notes from that [first] meeting: Next to my comment about leadership is the word *informal* in parentheses.
>
> At this point I see that I was in a transitional stage. I viewed myself as a teacher who had influence over other people, a kind of de facto leader, but I hadn't yet acknowledged or come to a full realization of my formal role as a leader in our school. What I will document in my portfolio is my transitional journey, which is to a large degree the journey of how I have come to accept myself as a legitimate, formal school leader. Underpinning this

self acceptance is the confidence I have developed in myself as a leader. . . . (*Ceilah* 5/93)

## Habits of Reflection
## Will Make Me a Better Leader

The final outcome relating to members' self-knowledge was a new or renewed commitment to reflection as a means of developing their effectiveness as leaders. For many, discovering new ways to think about themselves and their behaviors as leaders was a major breakthrough. For example, Bonnie, a teacher leader, compared her new approach to leadership with her previous "just blundering along":

> I need to be more introspective, self-analytical, and self-critical. Only by being reflective on an intrapersonal level can I truly find out what's happening with me, growth-wise. In the past it was too easy to just "do it," not worry about *why* or its impact. I would just blunder along, not being very sensitive to the influence my actions would have on others.
>
> I am now so much more self-aware. . . . [My S&D Team has been instrumental in helping me develop this self-awareness.] Best of all, I know they'll be behind me, pushing, pushing, pushing [in the future]. They won't let me fail! (*Bonnie* 8/92)

Members often credited the reflective practice structures of the Academy—the LDP, the I-C-I framework, the S&D Team, the facilitators, and specific activities—for this growth. As the Academy ended, many vowed to continue these on their own or in small groups.

MASL members found in newly acquired habits of reflection a mechanism for managing their feelings of being overwhelmed by the demands of leadership. Like school leaders elsewhere, these Maine leaders felt burdened by the physical and emotional exhaustion of running their schools, spearheading a reform, or alleviating negativism and defeatism among colleagues. MASL's attention to the intrapersonal domain helped them to stay in touch with themselves. It legitimized the role of personal feelings, philosophies, and physical stamina in shaping their abilities to lead. This focused some members on "new habits" of thinking, acting, and organizing their professional lives to keep their personal lives "healthy." One fourth grade teacher who was the president of the teachers' association, for example, set a goal of working "only a 55-hour work week," down from 65-plus hours. He, like many others, strived to discipline himself and his work environment so that he could "be a whole person" and thereby be a more effective educator and leader, parent and spouse.

Time for reflection and introspection was often seen as key to maintaining perspective on these things. At the end of the Academy, most members were far less worried than at the start about their technical knowledge of education programs and techniques. They tended, instead, to focus on keeping a balanced perspective on interpersonal relationships at school and staying in touch with their own purposes, competencies, and limits. Margaret, an elementary principal, expressed it well:

> The last 7 months, with the support of my Academy colleagues, have given me the unique opportunity to focus inward. I am learning more and more each day about [myself as] educator, business woman, friend, sister, and colleague.
>
> These learnings are not isolated to my Academy work or my professional work at Carver. Rather my eyes and ears are open daily to how I am acting, reacting, communicating, using information, and dealing with feedback. These learnings are neither grand nor elaborate. They are small bits that will add to some very important skills, attitudes, feelings, and abilities in my future.
>
> I don't need another project put in place to be a more effective leader. I don't need to worry about what to do with my staff members or board members. What I do need is a continuing look inward, an honest evaluation of *my* skills, attitudes, and beliefs. Learning to lead myself is my first step to more effective leadership at Carver School.
>
> The Academy has given me a voice. My S&D Team and my Academy colleagues have allowed and encouraged me to be open and, at times, vulnerable. I have tried to capture these feelings in my memory as I want to foster it with my own staff and our Administrative Council. . . . I am going to rely on the feedback and support. (*Margaret 8/92*)

Journal writing, reading, meditation, walking and other forms of regular exercise, and protecting time for family and self became part of many members' routines during the Academy. Most important, with the assistance of one another, these Maine leaders learned how these sorts of activities could help them as people and as leaders. Ed, an elementary principal, noted that his writing eventually allowed him to get past criticizing what others' were doing in his school and to address what he could do about it. Bill, a teacher leader, developed the following mantra to keep him focused on self-reflection:

> It was working on the intrapersonal—reflect, write, share, and revise—that developed my ability to look at myself as a leader. This was the most important aspect of my leadership growth. . . . And I continue to ask the key question, "Am I growing as a leader?" (*Bill* 6/93)

## Summary:
## Leading Better Starts
## With Knowing Myself Better

In the final analysis, Bill's question captures the essence of the growth experienced by most MASL members. Over the course of the Academy, they developed a clearer view of what leading meant and how they were functioning as leaders. Their journeys expanded their understanding of the leadership needs of their schools. They also came to know their own personal qualities, styles, and skills more concretely and to see more clearly how they affected other people. Then, through taking risks to change specific behaviors with others at school, they came to feel that they could both influence others in a purposeful way and continue to grow as leaders.

At the outset of the Academy, many participants wondered, "Am I a leader in my school?" At its close, most were asking Bill's question: "Am I growing as a leader?" The transition from uncertainty about role to pushing the envelope of their own effectiveness captures the story of many. Although the proof of their effects has yet to be established, all but a few MASL members are convinced that their inner journeys enabled them to begin behaving in their schools in ways that will ultimately benefit children's learning.

# LEARNING AS WE LEAD
## Creating a Culture for
## Learning and Community

A year at it has integrated the I-C-I framework into my being. I
will never be the same person again. I've reflected a lot about all
three dimensions and their interaction. It was very powerful for
me. The process of reflecting and planning and especially the
weaving of dimensions together in thought and action [will
shape everything I do as a school leader].

*Orin 6/93*

We began this book with two purposes. First, we were searching in
the developmental stories of our 58 Academy colleagues to understand better how leaders extend and deepen their positive influence
in their schools. Second, we wondered how the MASL model for
leadership development might stimulate and support the extension
and deepening of such influence.

The preceding chapters have recounted experiences common to
most MASL members' journeys toward leadership growth. Certainly, these journeys took our Maine colleagues into risky spots,
challenged most of them to find resources within themselves, and
forged bonds among them as they worked through these challenges
together. But the MASL experience left us less certain that these
developmental journeys had, in fact, affected the learning of students in these travelers' schools.

In this final chapter, we highlight two sets of lessons about the process of leadership growth that we—staff and members alike—have drawn from this experience. We offer them not as definitive advice, for the practical outcomes from MASL do not yet merit solid conclusions. Our lessons are more like discoveries we found ourselves "rediscovering" throughout the Academy and the writing of this book. Through their repetition, we have come to trust these discoveries more and more and to feel they should be shared with others who are working on their own leadership growth or to promote such growth among others.

We begin with five lessons about leadership growth and then share four observations about the environment that might foster these. We close with a short reflection on the nature of school leadership.

## Five Not-So-Easy
## Lessons About Leadership Growth

The action of leadership is so rapid, varied, and interpersonally complex that learning how well we are leading is extraordinarily difficult. The Academy gave our members a rare opportunity to learn from real dilemmas they faced as leaders and to mold from them new leadership strategies they could put to work immediately. But this process led them into a quagmire of old ideas about leadership, old habits of leadership and followership, and existing relationships with people who seemed to prefer that they act in old ways. Time was always short and the energy to change both themselves and others was even shorter.

In the face of the extraordinary challenge of *acting differently at work,* the temptation to be satisfied only with new insights and ideas was strong indeed. Without help from one another in their schools, most Academy members would not have progressed toward the goal of affecting students. We offer the following not-so-easy lessons as suggestions for making learning lead to new action.

### Have a Plan That
### Targets Better Student Learning

We learned that targeting *student* outcomes has a centering effect on leaders as they plunge into the morass of leadership issues.

Throughout the Academy, members found it extraordinarily difficult to grasp precisely how their leadership was becoming more—or
less—effective. As MASL leaders swam more deeply into the details
and dynamics of their own schools, colleagues, and selves, the
number of ways they could improve as leaders seemed to grow
exponentially. Repeatedly confirming that a link existed between
their LDPs and enhanced learning outcomes for children reassured
members and kept their precious efforts to grow focused on a
meaningful, if elusive, target.

The target itself served an important function. It was so difficult
to see the effects of one's behaviors on children that members were
constantly inclined to dwell instead on the labyrinth of intervening
effects. It took such energy to shift, for example, a teacher leader's
interactions with her principal that she could easily lose track of the
student outcomes she sought to affect in the process. The Academy's
explicit and sometimes tortuous attention to leaders' effects on
student learning brought such efforts back to their basic purpose.
Focusing on student learning sustained members by allowing them
to see an honorable goal for often arduous and ambiguous work.

This target then gave members an articulable rationale for steps
they took to strengthen their leadership. Being clear about the target
helped a plan for leadership growth to emerge. The LDP format,
structured with intersecting cognitive, interpersonal, and intrapersonal goals, helped members to specify behavioral changes with
others designed to influence school practices so that student learning would demonstrably improve. These plans guided and steadied
members' efforts as a keel assures a sailboat's way.

### Change Begins With You

The sometimes tortuous path in search of a starting point for
school and leadership improvement brought most of our leaders back,
eventually, to themselves. We found that they could more easily affect
permanent change in themselves than in a whole school or in specific
people. If conditions permitted, we discovered, changes in the leaders
themselves could trigger changes in others and eventually in the
school. The Academy gave its members time, personal support, and
permission to bring the change process home to themselves.

We were amazed at how members found this process personally
and professionally affirming. It allowed them to shed old beliefs that

leadership resided outside of themselves and beyond their control. Instead, members learned to see leadership as a capacity for influencing the school that resided within each of them. Their development as leaders became a matter of how they wanted to nurture this capacity intellectually, interpersonally, and behaviorally.

In this vein, we confirmed Tom Sergiovanni's (1992) notion that leading engages head, heart, *and* hands. MASL members rapidly learned that their schools would not change simply because they had learned a new idea, theory, or program strategy. They discovered that their schools would respond when they began to *behave* differently. To succeed at doing so, their beliefs and values—their "hearts"—needed to be aligned with these new actions and ideas. Although "head," or cognitive, changes often came quite easily, "heart" changes, or changes in their beliefs, commitments, and their interpersonal relationships, came with more difficulty. "Hands" changes, or changes to their behaviors, often needed to be preceded by the other two. Many members found that understanding these differences through the I-C-I model gave them an added sense of order, their leadership strategies a clearer purpose, and tools for assessing how their leadership activities affected others and themselves.

### Trust Yourself . . . and Your Colleagues

Some of the most powerful moments for MASL members and their school colleagues came from "leveling" with one another about their feelings. Many came to the Academy trailing behind them doubts or even guilt about the effectiveness of their working relationships with staff, colleagues, boss, parents, and even students. Everyone believed he or she was failing as a leader with someone! It often turned out that sharing this concern with the problematic person or group at school in a constructive way actually started the process of improvement. The first step for many was to confront the conflict. Then they could communicate "more authentically" with the truculent janitor, the faculty who took little responsibility, or the supervisor who unknowingly belittled a teacher leader.

We were struck by the number of Academy members who felt trapped by traditional leadership expectations. Their own images of who they should be and how they should act were shaped powerfully by the "in charge" administrative leader model. And most, including principals, found that this model was neither healthy for their schools nor for themselves as individuals. The Academy encouraged them to seek and to develop authentic styles of their own—to trust that they could lead. By exploring their strengths and weaknesses and being realistic about these with others, MASL leaders often grew more comfortable and confident. This in turn freed them to be more open and collaborative with others.

In this way, members' leadership came to reflect their own personalities and value systems, not someone else's. They turned an "honest eye" on themselves and became clearer about what they could and could not, and would and would not, do as leaders. Sharing this knowledge helped their colleagues understand better what MASL leaders did and why. It permitted them as well to specify how they needed help from those colleagues. Being more authentic as a leader thus helped everyone "clear the air" of uncertainties, conflicts, and misunderstandings—and to focus themselves as an individual, a team, a faculty, and a community on their primary work with children.

### Listen to People You Seek to Lead

This sense of realism about themselves and the leadership positions they occupied or aspired to was, we believe, an exceptionally important outcome of the Academy. With it, our leaders were equipped to find compatible ways to lead and to imprint consciously on their leadership roles the styles and priorities they could in fact deliver on. They were also prepared to enlist help and expertise from others in those areas for which their own leadership was lacking. A prime result of feeling better about themselves as leaders was that they felt more control over themselves and over their work.

The commitment to learn together and the "safety net" of the Academy made frank and open self-assessment a common occurrence. Academy colleagues helped one another fill in the picture of themselves in action as leaders. With feedback on their actions from people they could trust, members became surer of their strengths and weaknesses. These relationships also made it possible to address some tough questions: Why is it that I fall into these patterns with people who overextend me? How effective can I really be at all these things, with all these people? Why do I feel responsible for them? How can I work *with and through* other people more?

We have come to see the network of relationships within MASL as a precondition for addressing challenging leadership issues at school. It helped many members summon the courage to listen more attentively to those they wanted to influence there. Feedback and support from MASL colleagues allowed them to ask for feedback from colleagues at school. Such consultation often transformed relationships with those colleagues, in effect making leadership more authentic, widely shared, and manageable.

### Choose to Lead

Finally, we learned the vast importance of actively choosing to lead. We learned this most poignantly from the MASL members who started the Academy *not* feeling they were leaders. Most often, these were teachers who thought of themselves as interlopers or ghost leaders functioning in the backchannels of the school. Even some principals, despite their formal positions and vast activities, did not see themselves "really" influencing their schools' educational success with children.

These members (who probably constituted a majority of the Academy) found that the feeling of leading grew from the act of choosing to lead. The LDP was often the vehicle for this act of choosing; it made members select a student outcome target, a series of interpersonal "means" to influence it, and some intrapersonal changes that would initiate it all. The LDP forced them to take a lead in one or two arenas of school life that were demonstrably important to children's learning. This often forced them to back off from less productive (but very busy) activity in many other arenas. As Bill put it, "If I hadn't gone through the Academy, I'd have 16 titles by now and wouldn't be an effective leader in any of them" (*Bill* 6/93).

Making the choice to lead set off a cycle that kept reinforcing leadership behaviors. The LDP formalized this choice and specified actions to be taken. Simply having that plan and the encouragement to act upon it led to some form of action. In turn, assessing their actions in journal writing, discussions with critic-friends, and feedback from colleagues often helped members see specific effects as well as next steps. Confidence grew from small risks, trustworthy feedback, and evidence of success. Finally, stronger confidence permitted more accurate and sensible future choices about when, how, and with whom members should exert influence. In most cases, a cycle of small planned risks and reflective interludes fed itself into a productive upward spiral of growth.

## The Nurturing of Leaders' Growth

MASL staff and members learned as much about the conditions that encourage growth as we did about leadership growth itself. We have documented some of these in our *Curriculum Packet* (Donaldson et al., 1993) as has the external evaluation (Johnson et al., 1993). We will briefly describe here four discoveries about the learning environment for school leadership growth that emerged from the Academy experience.

### Leaders Learn Best in Their Schools

Our experience reinforced repeatedly the observation that the essence of leadership lies in acts of leadership and the effects those have on others. Learning, then, must take place where those "acts" are—in the school. Throughout the 16 months, MASL members were asked, encouraged, and directed to assess their leadership needs and to formulate their leadership goals around the real students, adults, and programs of their own schools. They then tried to *act more effectively* with those students, adults, and programs and sought feedback and consultation from S&D Teams, facilitators, and colleagues at school. Clearly, this could not have happened if their schools had not been a major theater for Academy activity.

Without the school's reality base, it would have been exceptionally difficult to build and sustain a focus on leadership *effects*, a focus essential to leaders' self-assessment, planning, action, and evaluation. Often, classes or workshops on leadership, lacking access to the acts and effects, focus instead on models for ideal leadership action and planning for action. These are, as Ed put it, "conceived in wonderful vacuum" and usually fail to accommodate the realities of people and relationships that surround leaders at school.

MASL placed the focus on leaders' *behaviors at work* and kept asking, "How do your behaviors influence what others are thinking, valuing, and doing here?" and "How might they improve so students will benefit?" As Academy members became more skilled at answering these questions for themselves, we believe their leadership effectiveness increased. Because leadership happens at school, it stands to reason that most leadership growth happens there as well. Most leaders need help to bring the lessons of that growth to fruition.

## Protect and Foster Self-Reflection

We learned in MASL that the vast majority of our leaders thirsted for an opportunity to make sense out of what was happening to themselves as leaders and as people. Certainly, some of this was prompted by the chaotic and embattled nature of school improvement in the 1990s. But much was as well motivated by a need to know how well they were leading so they could see more clearly how they could improve as leaders.

Programs can begin to quench this thirst by giving leaders a major responsibility in shaping their own learning and by building a psychologically and philosophically safe environment for them. Self-assessment instruments, autobiographical works by school leaders, observations and consultations from colleagues and staff after role-plays and "mock" leadership situations, and feedback from colleagues at work can sharpen the image in each leader's mirror. Learning what it meant to be a Myers-Briggs "extrovert," for example, helped some members understand how they were probably being perceived by others at work. That knowledge helped them devise strategies for communicating with others and carrying out other leadership tasks in a more successful manner. Often, Academy colleagues, the S&D Team, and staff provided a safer interpersonal environment for learning about these things and for trying on new behaviors than their schools could provide.

Busy leaders simply cannot stop the action long enough to see themselves accurately. Consequently, self-development efforts cannot begin with a reasonably accurate picture of strengths, weaknesses, styles, or habits. A leadership development program can protect time and space and offer a colleague-critic culture to foster self-understanding. These, we found, are the most essential ingredients for growth.

## Nurture Interpersonal Learning and Action

If leadership "begins with me," it "happens through others." MASL members confirmed through their own developmental journeys what we all intuitively know about schools: They are organizations that operate almost completely on human capacity; their leadership depends almost totally on *interpersonal factors*. This confirmation resulted from our program's ability to help members recognize, assess, plan, and act in the interpersonal dimension.

MASL taught us that interpersonal learning can happen on at least two levels: intellectual and experiential. Many members benefited from didactic presentations of, for instance, interpersonal communication theory, group dynamics, or conflict management concepts and strategies. But it was more powerful to be placed in leadership settings, asked to act, and then analyze and reflect on those actions with other participants. MASL did this by role-plays, simulations, observing members at work in their schools, and "rehearsing" new behaviors prior to using them at school. Learning from one's own "behavioral data" was often extraordinarily rewarding. The crucial role of colleagues in providing feedback was often enhanced by three factors: the intimacy and honesty of the S&D Team and/or with the facilitator; the long duration of the Academy; and the multiplicity of perspectives provided by our mixed membership of teachers and administrators.

Interpersonal leadership challenges have a certain universal quality. Building trust, clarifying meaning, establishing common purpose, facilitating mutually agreeable decisions, and resolving conflicts or hurt feelings are constant interpersonal activities for school leaders. The leadership development program that helps a leader improve in one of these functions builds in that leader a new capacity that will operate throughout his or her work.

## Make the Program Follow the Learning (Not Vice Versa)

The Maine Academy adhered pretty faithfully to the principle that adult learning is a self-initiated and self-paced process that works best in a collaborative, interdependent "learning community." Academy staff also believed that effective school leaders are model learners; their conduct needs to exemplify for everyone the central learning activities and purposes of the school. MASL staff attempted to model this function themselves by simultaneously challenging members to identify and pursue their own leadership growth goals and supporting them unequivocally in their efforts.

This characteristic of MASL drew extensive praise (and, at various times, frustration, exhaustion, and even anger) from our members. We have emerged from the MASL experience convinced that leadership development programs must see their function as helping leaders to engage in *learning from which they draw meaning and purpose.* Such programs force educational leaders to confront their own assumptions and practices as leaders and as learners. From the struggles inherent in this confrontation, if appropriate support and resources are present, they can emerge with a more coherent philosophy not only for leadership but for modeling learning for teachers, students, administrators, parents, and everyone else in the school community.

We found that, for a program to do this, it must start with the learner, not with a preconceived curriculum (which must necessarily make some assumptions about what all leaders need to learn). It must structure activities to simultaneously permit participants to investigate effective leadership and to question their real and potential capacity to be such a leader. Because this is intrusive, sometimes risky, and tremendously engaging work for most leaders, a program must support each individual and be ready to respond with resources, challenging questions, and faith in him or her. In the final analysis, a program needs to approach its work with school leaders in precisely the same manner that it would hope those leaders would approach their work leading their schools.

## Conclusion:
## And So It Goes . . . and Goes . . .

We began our book with the hope that readers would find that it engaged their own ambitions to become better school leaders or nurturers of school leaders. If you are like us, you have been touched most by the words of our Maine colleagues. Despite the months that have passed since the Academy formally transitioned into a looser network, we have been repeatedly struck by the intensity and the enduring personal nature of this process called leadership growth.

We are left with a deepening respect both for these educators and for the complexity of the quest for improved leadership. To lead is difficult enough; to dare to improve how one leads threatens to overtax every personal and professional resource. We have come to appreciate the long-term nature of the quest to lead more effectively. Just as leaders cannot will their schools to improve themselves, neither can they simply will themselves to become better leaders.

The process is inexact and requires repeated forays into new ideas, beliefs, and behaviors followed by periods of reflection and analysis. It is an iterative process, as we found through repeated "cycling through" the LDP planning sequence. It follows that progress is likely to be terribly incremental, small step by small step, as new behaviors prove useful or not and as the school environment demonstrates this utility. So teachers, principals, and citizens anxious to lead more effectively will need to persist in their efforts to influence and be tireless in monitoring the effects of that influence.

These qualities of the leadership development process suggest the ineffectiveness of staff development promising quick fixes and "repair kit" courses that claim to make better leaders overnight. If leadership improvement requires leaders to be in it for the long haul, then it stands to reason that universities, school districts, and leadership development programs must stand by those leaders for the long haul. School leaders themselves seem to understand the complexities and incremental qualities of this professional journey. We hope our book has inspired them to create within their professional associations and their schools new services and conditions to promote their growth. The future success of their schools and the students in them demand nothing less.

# APPENDIX

The Appendix includes documents used repeatedly in the Maine Academy for School Leaders and referred to in this book. They appear here in the form we used them. For further details, see Donaldson, Marnik, Martin, and Barnes (1993).

# Examining My Leadership

*A Diagnostic Framework Leading
to Setting Personal and Professional
Learning Goals to Enhance Leadership*

## Our Assumptions

Leadership occurs in a human medium. It requires both leader(s) and "led"; the medium in which it happens are the relationships, purposes, and dreams existing among people as they work together in the school. We cannot understand or affect leadership without understanding that medium as well as the leader(s) and the group (the led). Improving how we lead requires that we know better the medium, the group, and ourselves and that we learn how to use this knowledge to alter our individual and collective behavior.

## Three Questions

### I. What is my ideal/model leader like?

Focus on IDEALS.

Begin by asking: What is it that I value in a good leader? What is the blueprint I carry around with me and use to evaluate leaders and their organizations?

Leadership ideals usually include images of a *person,* a *group,* and the *medium or organizational context* in which they interact to move their school forward. These are the intrapersonal, interpersonal, and cognitive dimensions of your ideal.

Think of the following:

- Models and philosophies that show how successful leadership works (C)
- Models for how effective learning and schools work (C)
- Interpersonal behaviors you associate with successful leaders and successfully led groups (In)

- Personality/dispositions/backgrounds/talents of people who are successful leaders (IA)

## II. How do the relationships among people in my school help or hinder my leadership?

Focus on ADULTS, CHILDREN, AND HOW YOU ARE ORGANIZED in light of the IDEAL.

What kinds of groups exist at school and how are they structured?

Begin by asking: How does my type of organization enable and constrain certain models of leadership? What do Maine schools and communities expect in a leader? What do they need?

The interpersonal context is shaped by the way the school is organized, the nature of the work people do, the culture of past practices and norms, and the expectations of the community and state.

Think of the following:

- How the school systematically treats students and how this affects their success (C)
- The formal structures of roles, schedules, curriculum, policies that shape student outcomes (C)
- The informal networks of relationships, subgroups, past practices, and personal histories that establish norms for how people think and behave (In)
- Expectations of the leader by students, staff, parents, and supervisors (I-C-I)
- The demands these place on you (IA)

## III. What capabilities do I have/not have that will enable me to succeed as a leader for my school?

Focus on YOURSELF—and then on YOURSELF in your ORGANIZATIONAL CONTEXT seeking your IDEAL.

Begin by asking: Do I have what it takes? How can I develop what it takes?

Your capabilities include your interpersonal style, skills, and habits (In), your knowledge and beliefs about the work of schools, leadership and teaching/learning (C), and your ability to monitor and adjust how you act with others for the benefit of the group, the other person(s), and yourself (IA).

Think of the following:

- How comfortable you are speaking, thinking, and acting "in front" of others (IA)
- How well others listen to and understand you and you listen to and understand others (In)
- How broad your knowledge is about teaching, learning, and human development is (C)
- How clear you are about what is good for children, adults, and their learning (C)
- How tolerant you are of alternative philosophies, personalities, and work/life styles (In and C)
- How comfortable you are acknowledging what you don't know and cannot do and seeking assistance from others publicly (IA)
- How well you share responsibility and structure participation in decisions and problem solving accordingly (In and IA)

# The Leadership Development Plan Synopsis

Use this as a planning device for your LDP. Your plans for developing your leadership should address all three dimensions of leadership. You can begin from any dimension but need to consider how the needs and goals you choose in that dimension have implications and "partners" in the other two.

| | INTRAPERSONAL GOALS to support | INTERPERSONAL GOALS to support | TASK/PROGRAM GOALS (cognitive) |
|---|---|---|---|
| **G O A L S** | 1.<br>2.<br>3. | 1.<br>2.<br>3 | 1.<br>2.<br>3. |
| **A S S E S S M E N T** | What *assessment* of your needs as a person supports these goals? ⇒ | What *assessment* of your school's "people needs" supports these goals? ⇒ | What *assessment* of your school's effectiveness (related to student outcomes) supports these goals? |
| **P L A N  T O  G R O W** | The ways you will *shape your behaviors, thoughts, and feelings* to prepare for ⇒<br><br>What are your plans to reach these goals? (Be specific and realistic.) | the ways you will *work with others* to<br><br>What are your plans to reach these goals? (Be specific and realistic.) | have the *school work differently with children/constituents* so that ⇒ student learning is improved.<br><br>What are your plans to reach these goals? (Be specific and realistic.) |
| **E V A L U A T I O N** | How will you evaluate whether you've reached your goals? (What feedback loops do you need for what types of information?) ⇒ | How will you evaluate whether you've reached your goals? (What feedback loops do you need for what types of information?) ⇒ | How will you evaluate whether you've reached your goals? (What feedback loops do you need for what types of information?) |

NOTE: The logical connections among the three dimensions need to be clear: How will your intrapersonal skill goals put you in a better position to reach your interpersonal goals and programmatic goals? How will your interpersonal goals help you reach your program goals? See "The Leadership Development Project," "Examining My Leadership," and "Curriculum Scheme" for details.

# Curriculum Scheme

| Three Dimensions | Assessment | | Planning the Leadership Development Plan | Evaluation for Portfolio/Exhibition |
|---|---|---|---|---|
| Interpersonal (In) | My relationships to others; to social/ organizational realities of my school | 1 to 1<br>1 to task group<br>1 to faculty<br>1 to public | Specific strategies for relating differently to individuals and groups to accomplish goals in "C." | Observation and feedback from others; reflective journals |
| Cognitive (C) | My ideals, values, ideas about leading and education | learning<br>teaching<br>curriculum<br>leader<br>follower<br>ends/means | Specific strategies to acquire new concepts and share them with others in shaping programs and practices for enhanced student outcomes. | Student outcomes and staff/school performance data |
| Intrapersonal (Ia) | My knowledge of myself | skills<br>personality<br>talents<br>emotions<br>goals<br>needs | Specific strategies for shaping my behaviors, thoughts, feelings, and beliefs to accomplish "In" and "C" goals. | Reflection; consultation with trusted others; observation and feedback |

LEADERSHIP

BEHAVIORS

AND

BELIEFS

# Assessing Our S&D's
# Activities and Process

Instructions:

Think back over the way your S&D Team has typically operated in the past few months. Then rate it on each of the following aspects of group activity, using this rating scheme:

1—Never
2—Rarely
3—Sometimes
4—Often
5—Always
NA—Not Appropriate

## Our S&D Team:

a. _____ Meets often enough to be helpful to me.
b. _____ Meets on time (starting and ending).
c. _____ Operates from an agenda known to all members ahead of time.
d. _____ Sticks to its ground rules.
e. _____ Gives me useful, specific feedback.
f. _____ Gives useful, specific feedback to all other members.
g. _____ Makes me feel supported.
h. _____ Makes all other members feel supported.
i. _____ Challenges me to try harder to improve my leadership.
j. _____ Challenges all other members to try harder to improve their leadership.
k. _____ Has members who share equally the responsibility for making the group a success.
l. _____ Stays focused on the task.
m. _____ Provides all members a place to be listened to.
n. _____ Helps all members understand their work and themselves better.
o. _____ Leaves me with a sense of being valued and replenished.
p. _____ Encourages differences of opinion and conflicting advice among its members.

q. _____ Enjoys itself.
r. _____ Has a high level of commitment from all its members.
s. _____ Is a useful resource to me in my work as a leader.
t. _____ Helps me stay focused on my LDP by suggesting specific ways to improve my leadership.
u. _____ Pays appropriate attention to its "creature comforts" so that meetings are pleasant.
v. _____ Has full participation from all members.

Other Reactions I Might Like to Share With the Team:

# A Portfolio of Leadership Learning

## *Purposes*

The purposes of the Portfolio of Leadership Learning are the following:

1. To show that you have identified appropriate and specific knowledge and behaviors (in your LDP goals) that you need to improve to become a more effective leader.
2. To show what you have done to improve these over the past 14 months.
3. To show how your understanding and practice of these has evolved over the period.

The Portfolio consists of two types of materials: documentation and narrative. The documentation makes the story that the narrative tells come alive with vivid detail.

## *Documentation of Goals, Activities, and Impacts*

These are evidence of your goals, your activities to improve your leadership, and your success at reaching them. We suggest you organize it around each major LDP goal and the impact LDP activities had on you, your colleagues, and your school's student outcomes.

Within the story of each goal, we suggest three chronological phases be documented:

*Phase I—Where I Started*

- Application to MASL
- Examining My Leadership
- Journal entries
- Early LDP drafts
- Assessment around the need for and baseline data on the cognitive/task and interpersonal dimensions of your early goals

*Phase II—Where I've Been*

- Successive LDP drafts
- LDP synopsis and entry plans
- Journal entries

- Examples of reflection on practice (e.g., see January 23 session)
- Periodic "taking stock" self- and other assessments
- S&D Team Agreement
- Reactions to meaningful readings, workshops, and other experiences (see summer institute notes)
- *And especially* "data" from colleagues, the facilitator, and your S&D Team that tells you something significant about your leadership:
  - several observations by colleagues, S&D Team members, and facilitators and your reflections on what you learned from this feedback
  - feedback from various constituencies (e.g., staff, parents, students, others)
  - samples of your leadership in action (audiotapes, videotapes) *and* reflections
  - evidence of changes in targeted student outcomes

*Phase III—Where I Am Now*

- Most recent refocused LDP, with explanation for current goals and plans
- Journal entries
- Feedback from others collected in the past 6 weeks to help focus your LDP (see Phase II)

## Written Narrative of Learning About My Leadership

Think of this as a reflection on your "journey" as a learner these past 12 to 14 months in the Academy. The territory you've journeyed through is made up of your experiences in the Academy and, most important, in your job as you've used your LDP to make yourself a better leader.

The documentation you've assembled is your collection of "souvenirs" and "log entries" from that journey. The written narrative is what sense you make of where you've been and what that means about where you'll "go" next. You might think of it as your retrospective "guided tour" through your learning about your leadership . . . and your best ideas about the "path" immediately before you.

The narrative can be located in one place in your Portfolio or, preferably, broken into sections by LDP goals or by the phases described above. In either case, the documentation that goes with each section of narrative should be close by and well referenced in the narrative.

In writing the narrative, look back and write about important . . .

> places where you've gotten a "good view" of yourself, your school (or place of work), the leadership needs of that place and the people in it. These are insights into the interrelationships between you, your workplace, and your skills as a leader.

- What happened? What was the insight or discovery?
- What did you discover about your capacity to lead?
- What did you discover about your limitations as a leader?
- Who and what helped you gain this insight?

> "bumps" along the way . . . experiences, periods of time, conversations, Academy activities when you felt perplexed, uncertain, discouraged about what you were doing as a leader. These might represent the challenges you face in extending your leadership skills and knowledge.

- What was most perplexing about these? What questions do they lead to about yourself, your school or organization, and your skills and knowledge as a leader there?
- What is your understanding now of these challenging questions? What are possible "leads" for you to follow to meet those challenges?

Again, use documentation to illustrate what you've learned . . . for example, by referencing your journal entry from a certain date, by referring to an entry in your periodic taking stock assessment of growth or to an event that you discussed with your S&D Team or facilitator.

### Where I Will Go From Here

Conclude your Portfolio with a section in which you look forward and write about *where I will go from here* in my journey toward improved leadership.

You might explore:

- The kind of leader I can best be (What kind or kinds? In what kinds of settings? With what sorts of people?)
- The aspects of "you" that will need to be sustained and strengthened that make you a successful leader
- The aspects that will need to be "kept in check"
- Your plans for tending to these aspects of "you" in the next 6 months to a year, including the assistance you'll need from people

you live with, work with, and regard as helpful to your professional growth

### *A Few Helpful Hints*

Portfolio materials should relate directly to your LDP. If you have a lot of items related to other facets of your professional life, save them, reflect on them, frame them, impress your boss with them, or just feel good about them. But please don't include them in your Portfolio. Thanks!

Quality, not quantity, continues to be the Academy's primary criterion for success. A few carefully chosen examples that show your professional growth and reflection and change over time are vital. You need not make the Portfolio a description of *every* Academy moment or activity. Include the parts of your MASL work that speak to the three or four leadership behaviors you were trying to change.

You are repeatedly experiencing professional growth. Taking a small amount of time to connect what you just learned to an LDP goal will help you build your Portfolio as you go along.

GOOD LUCK !!!!!

# REFERENCES

Angelou, M. (1993). *On the pulse of morning.* NY: Random House.

Argyris, C., & Schön, D. (1974). *Theory in practice.* San Francisco: Jossey-Bass.

Barth, R. (1991). *Improving schools from within.* San Francisco: Jossey-Bass.

Covey, S. (1990). *The seven habits of highly effective people: Restoring the character ethic.* New York: Simon & Schuster.

Donaldson, G. A., Jr. (1993). *The nature of leadership knowledge and skills.* Unpublished manuscript. University of Maine.

Donaldson, G. A., Jr., Marnik, G., Martin, S., & Barnes, R. (1993). *Curriculum packet: A portfolio of materials explaining an innovative approach to leadership development.* Augusta: Maine Leadership Consortium.

Fullan, M. (1994). *The new meaning of educational change.* New York: Teachers College Press.

Fullan, M., & Hargreaves, A. (1991). *What's worth fighting for? Working together for your school.* Andover, MA: Regional Laboratory for the Educational Improvement of the Northeast and Islands.

Gardner, H. (1993). *Frames of mind* (2nd ed.). New York: Basic Books.

Hazzard, S. (1980). *Transit of Venus*. New York: Basic Books.

Hoffman, J., Mackenzie, S., McCabe, T., & McDonough, F. (1993). Developing leadership: Reflections of one S&D team's experience. *Reflections, 9*, 39-43.

Johnson, B., Morris, C. E., & Nicoletti, B. J. (1993). *Program evaluation: The Maine Academy for School Leaders*. Orono: Margaret Chase Smith Center for Public Policy, University of Maine.

Knowles, M. (1984). *Andragogy in action*. San Francisco: Jossey-Bass.

Levine, S. L. (1989). *Promoting adult growth in schools*. Boston: Allyn & Bacon.

Lieberman, A. (Ed.). (1988). *Building a professional culture in schools*. New York: Teachers College Press.

Little, J. W. (1986). Seductive images and organizational realities in professional development. In A. Lieberman (Ed.), *Rethinking school improvement* (pp. 26-44). New York: Teachers College Press.

McQuillan, P., & Muncey, D. (1993). Preliminary findings of a five year study of the Coalition of Essential Schools. *Phi Delta Kappan, 74*(6), 486-489.

Milstein, M. M., & Associates. (1993). *Changing the way we prepare educational leaders: The Danforth experience*. Newbury Park, CA: Corwin.

Murphy, J. (1988). The unheroic side of leadership: Notes from the swamp. *Phi Delta Kappan, 69*(9), 654-659.

Murphy, J. (1992). *The landscape of leadership preparation: Reframing the education of school administrators*. Newbury Park, CA: Corwin.

Osterman, K., & Kottkamp, R. (1993). *Reflective practice for educators: Improving schooling through professional development*. Newbury Park, CA: Corwin.

Schön, D. (1983). *The reflective practitioner*. New York: Basic Books.

Sergiovanni, T. (1992). *Moral leadership*. San Francisco: Jossey-Bass.

Wasley, P. A. (1991). *Teachers who lead*. New York: Teachers College Press.